Stock Market Investing for Newbies

Derek Chamberlain, MBA

For my wife, Carrie, who supported me while I wrote this book and my father who served as editor.

ISBN: Print 978-1500235277

TABLE OF CONTENTS

Products Included In This Book

Neither the author, nor the publisher, nor anyone involved with the creation of this book has a financial stake in any financial product mentioned in this book. No type of compensation of any kind is received from any of the products , services, or companies mentioned.

Accompanying Website

There is an accompanying website that discusses and features many of the concepts presented in this book. This personal finance website can be accessed for free at:

www.MoneyAhoy.com

PREFACE

Is there really a need for yet another beginner's book devoted to investing in the stock market?

I am glad you asked! There are a number of reasons that I felt it would be a good idea to add to the pile of stock market investment how-to books for investing newbies:

- **Too Complicated** – The stock market books I have surveyed are a bit too complicated and detailed for the newbie. I will try to cover the basics without getting too far into the weeds. I am trying to cover the most important 80% of what you need to know and leave the highly technical 20% out. The vast majority of us can get along with what I supply just fine! If you are really interested in picking up that extra 20%, you will need to continue your studies further.
- **Too Basic** – Other stock market books I have run across are way too basic. There are some eBooks out there on basic stock market investing that consist of only 25 pages. Really? I think 25 pages will hardly suffice for those of us that know next to nothing about stock market investing.
- **Poor Explanations** –I am not the most experienced stock market investor by any stretch of the imagination, but I think I have a small knack for explaining things in an easy to understand language. This should help you to get up to speed more quickly and leave fewer unanswered questions as you begin your journey of stock market investing.

- **Poor Accessibility** – I have found that so many people are interested in stock market investing, but do not know what concrete steps to take to get started with building their investment knowledge. Most investing books are simply not accessible for the reasons listed above. This book will give you step-by-step details and hold your hand through the entire stock market investing process.
- **Prevent Stunted Growth** – I wish that I would have had a simple book to help me learn more about stock market investing. If I had such a book to get me interested in investing in the stock market when I was around 15, I might be a multi-millionaire by now. Simply put, if even one person picks up or downloads this book and starts their investment journey as a result, I will consider my effort well spent.

I hope that as you read this book, you will find that I have struck a good balance between the points discussed above and developed a book that is accessible, actionable, and practical. I have tried to structure each chapter so you can quickly move through this book without getting bogged down in any one section. My goal is that you will be able to skim the sections containing information with which you are already familiar and spend more time learning about topics that are unfamiliar to you. My ultimate objective is to enable you to hit the ground running on your stock market investing journey when you finish this book.

Will this be the best stock market investing book for newbies ever written? Maybe not. But, it will help newbies with the basics and help them develop healthy stock market investing habits! Now, let's start our journey with Chapter 1 and a discussion of why you should even begin investing in the first place.

Chapter 1
WHY INVEST IN THE FIRST PLACE?

This chapter will convey why financial investments are so very important to your overall financial health. We will cover topics such as inflation, compound interest, typical long term investing results, and financial flexibility. If you are already familiar with these topics, you may want to skim ahead to Chapter-2.

1.1 - Inflation

There are two main reasons people seeking to improve their financial health invest in the stock market: inflation and compound interest. First, let's discuss inflation and learn more about this "hidden thief."

Wikipedia defines inflation as: "the persistent increase in the general price level of goods and services in an economy over a period of time." What the heck does this mean? Do you remember the story of how old granddad used to head down to the corner store when he was a kid and buy a soda-pop for a nickel? Today that same bottle of soda-pop will cost you $1.25 from a fancy vending machine!

If you do not save for the future yet get regular cost of living raises from your job, normal and steady inflation does not really matter all that much. You really do not have anything to lose. For savers like us, inflation really is the "hidden thief" that takes a little bit from our pockets each and every day. A penny here or a penny there is hard to notice over a couple of months. But, when you look back over the past 40 years it is surprising how much prices for normal everyday type of goods and services have increased. In recent years, inflation has been kept around the 2% - 4% range, but in Figure 1.1.1 you can see that annual inflation rates have been as high as 15%!

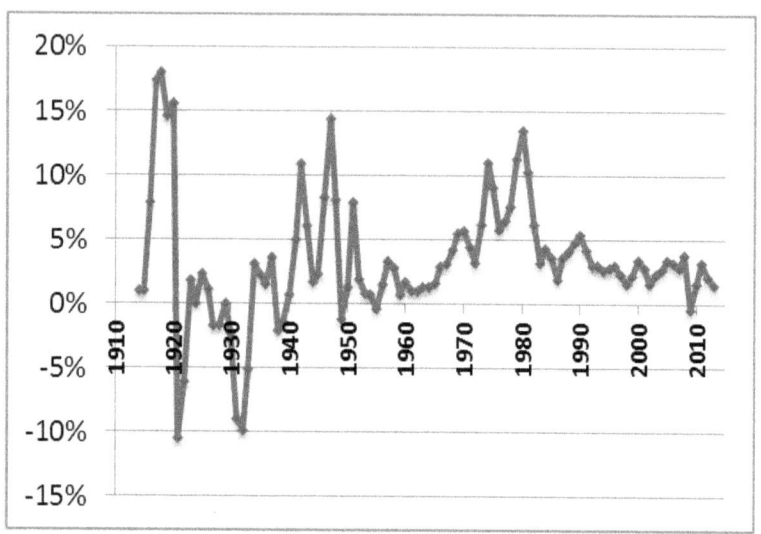

Figure 1.1.1 – Historical Rate of Inflation in the US
Bureau of Labor and Statistics - CPI data

Why is understanding the concept of inflation so important for people looking to increase their financial wealth?

Let's say you've just graduated college at the age of 22, and you're going to be very smart and save a little bit for retirement. You take a crisp new $100 bill from your first paycheck, take a long, sweet whiff of it, stick it in an old mason jar, crank down on the lid, and bury your treasure in a location known only to you. You then decide to dig up the secret jar 40 years later. On your first day of retirement, at the ripe age of 62, you are finally ready for the good life. You have slaved away for 40 years, and you are now ready for some good old rest and relaxation. Well, I am sorry to report that you'd be in for a bit of a surprise.

If inflation averaged 3% over those past 40 years, that $100 bill you stashed away would only be able to purchase about $31 of goods or services. How could that be? It's still the same $100 bill, right? Yes, you are technically correct. But, for the same reason your granddad only had to pay a nickel for a soda-pop, you will have to pay more than triple now for just about everything. That's what 40 years of inflation will do to your money if left stuck away in some old jar!

Aha! Just because inflation has been around 2% in the recent past doesn't mean it will stay that way in the future! That is true, but what if I told you that there were agencies in place that were created to guarantee a stable US currency.

What if I told you the US Federal Reserve (the FED) and the Federal Open Market Committee were created with a mandate to maintain price stability for goods and services? The FED maintains this price stability by targeting a 2% annual inflation rate. So you see, inflation is basically pre-programmed into our way of life by our central bank. Inflation is engineered into our everyday lives. There is really no practical way to avoid inflation.

If you want to build a sound financial future, you will need to find a way to at least break even with your savings. If you cannot do this, then every dollar you save for the future will end up losing most of its value over time.

To beat the "hidden thief" that is inflation, you need to find some type of income producing asset that will grow in value over time. There are a million and one things that a person could invest in that have the potential to increase in value over time. Just a couple examples include: old sports cars, violins, paintings, real estate, comic books, and other rare collectibles.

For the purposes of this book, I will discuss stock market investing.

Why is stock market investing such a good method for beating inflation?

As far back as financial records go, the stock market has increased in value and outpaced the rate of historical inflation. It is possible to prevent our savings from being eroded by inflation and also create considerable wealth over a lifetime.

1.2 - Compound Interest

Would anyone still want to invest in the stock market if inflation did not exist?

The answer is a resounding YES! Even if inflation did not exist, the effects of compound interest make it well worth one's time and effort to invest in the stock market. Let's explore why this is the case.

What the heck is compound interest and what will it do for me?

Hold onto your hats here, because things may get a little rough - I promise not to make this too complicated. According to Wikipedia **compound interest** occurs when: "interest is added to the principal of a deposit, so that, from that moment on, the interest that has been added also earns interest.

I will have to admit, that is a little dry even for me, and I'm an engineer! OK – let's see what I can do to clear things up.

One great way to help illustrate the principle of **compound interest** is with a neat little table (see Figure 1.2.1 below). Let's say that you invest $100 dollars in a stock that increases in value exactly 5% every year for 10 years. It is clear that every year you will earn five dollars on the principal amount that you invested ($100).

But, there is something more that you will earn in addition to the five dollars interest. Notice the column in Figure 1.2.1 titled "annual interest earned on the interest"? Each year you are earning 5% interest not only on the $100, but also on the previous year's interest that you have already been paid. So, in year number two, instead of just earning 5% interest on $100, you are earning 5% interest on $105!

Now, when you first get started investing, as in this example, that extra interest you'll earn is small (only 25 cents for year two of this example). But, if you follow along in Figure 1.2.1 below, you will notice something interesting about the annual interest earned on the interest.

Year	Starting Value	Annual Interest Earned on Principal	Annual Interest Earned on the Interest	Total Interest Earned	Annual Value
0	$100.00	$ -	$ -	$ -	$100.00
1	$100.00	$ 5.00	$ -	$ 5.00	$105.00
2	$100.00	$ 5.00	$ 0.25	$10.25	$110.25
3	$100.00	$ 5.00	$ 0.51	$15.76	$115.76
4	$100.00	$ 5.00	$ 0.79	$21.55	$121.55
5	$100.00	$ 5.00	$ 1.08	$27.63	$127.63
6	$100.00	$ 5.00	$ 1.38	$34.01	$134.01
7	$100.00	$ 5.00	$ 1.70	$40.71	$140.71
8	$100.00	$ 5.00	$ 2.04	$47.75	$147.75
9	$100.00	$ 5.00	$ 2.39	$55.13	$155.13
10	$100.00	$ 5.00	$ 2.76	$62.89	$162.89

TOTAL = $ 50.00 $ 12.89

Figure 1.2.1 – Compound Interest Example – 10 years

The fun thing with compound interest (I know – I am a math geek at heart) is that the "annual interest earned on the interest" literally tend to explode as you get farther out in years! As a neat little exercise, here is what that same table looks like when taken out 50 years (see Figure 1.2.2).

Notice that the compound interest component of $49.61 is nearly 10 times the interest that one would earn from just the principal ($5)! I hope you see where I am going with this. If not, that is OK! We will look at compound interest in a different way.

Year	Starting Value	Annual Interest Earned on Principal	Annual Interest Earned on the Interest	Total Interest Earned	Annual Value
0	$100.00	$ -	$ -	$ -	$ 100.00
1	$100.00	$ 5.00	$ -	$ 5.00	$ 105.00
2	$100.00	$ 5.00	$ 0.25	$ 10.25	$ 110.25
48	$100.00	$ 5.00	$ 44.53	$ 940.13	$1,040.13
49	$100.00	$ 5.00	$ 47.01	$ 992.13	$1,092.13
50	$100.00	$ 5.00	$ 49.61	$ 1,046.74	$1,146.74

TOTAL = **$ 250.00** **$ 796.74**

Figure 1.2.2 – Compound Interest Example – 50 years

I hope you will see from Figure 1.2.2 above that compound interest really begins to take off when you get further out in time (number of years). The compound interest effect on your investments also increases at a much faster rate as you achieve a higher percentage return on your investment. In Figure 1.2.3 below, you will find a chart for the investor that purchased $100 of stock with various percentage annual returns.

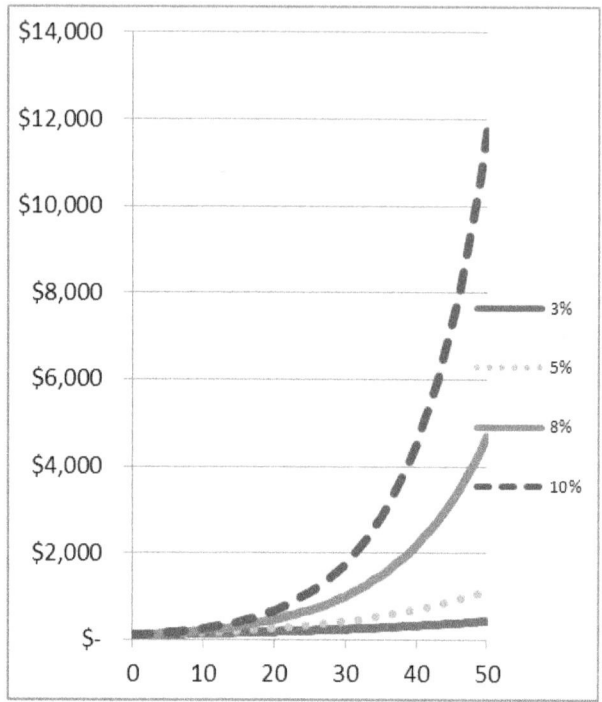

Figure 1.2.3 – Illustration of Compound Interest

Notice that the higher the annual percentage return, the more quickly the compound interest effect becomes significant. The initial $100 investment can literally go to the moon if left to compound long enough. As promised, if all of these tables, graphs, and such are a little confusing, let's look at a practical example that will reinforce the power of compound interest.

Let's take two great people: Smart Sally and Dumb Derek (no relation to me, of course). Smart Sally can afford to invest only **$400** a year into the stock market. Times are very tight for her, and she's made great sacrifices to find this amount to invest into the stock market. We will assume that she selects a moderate asset allocation and she achieves a 7% annual return on her investments.

Dumb Derek decides that the stock market is not for him. He is able to convince himself that it is just too risky and only for "gamblers." However, Dumb Derek is pretty good at saving. As a result, he is able to save a whopping **$2,000** each year. What does he do with his savings? He takes the ultra-conservative approach and decides to stuff it under his mattress. For this example, we will assume there is no inflation - 0% inflation for the next 50 years.

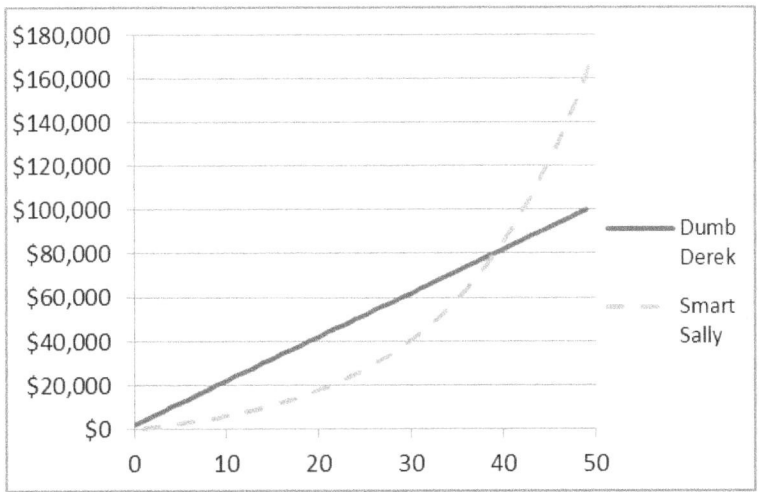

Figure 1.2.4 – Compound Interest Example
Smart Sally invests $400 a year at 7% interest; Dumb Derek saves $2,000 at 0% interest

Well, at the end of 50 years Dumb Derek has done pretty well for himself! He has been able to save a total of $100,000 ($2,000 a year times 50 years). Not too bad!

How about that Smart Sally? How can she expect to have much of a savings by only investing $400 a year into the stock market? At the end of 50 years, if she sells all of her investments, what would you guess she's been able to put away total? If you guessed something in the ballpark of $173,994.38, then you would be right!

Would you look at that? Even though Smart Sally was only investing **one fifth** of what Dumb Derek was saving each year, her wealth has accumulated to more than 1.7 times Derek's after 50 years! This is the awesome power of compound interest!

A neat rule of thumb that you can use to estimate the amount of time it will take your investments to double with compound interest is termed the rule of 72. You take the number 72 and divide it by the expected percent return. Thus, if we assume a 7% return from the stock market, you can expect your money to double roughly every 10 years (72/2 = 10.3 years). If you were able somehow to find investments that returned 10% annually, your money would double every 7.2 years (72/10 = 7.2). Pretty neat, huh?

One final thing I want to ensure you fully appreciate about compound interest is the tremendous power of time. Did you notice how it takes nearly 40 years for Smart Sally to catch up to Dumb Derek by investing only one fifth the amount that he does? However, after Smart Sally overtakes Dumb Derek, her savings begin to blow Dumb Derek's out of the water. Because time is such a crucial component when it comes to compounding interest, you will hear me preaching over and over again that it is essential to begin your stock market investing journey just as early as you can.

1.3 - Typical Stock Market Investing Results

Now that we have a better understanding of inflation and how compound interest works, we're ready to get down to business. Let's talk about what type of return on your investment you can expect out of the stock market over the long run. *What extra rate of return can we expect to earn by putting our money at increased risk in the stock market?*

Before we can answer that question, I need to lay a little more groundwork. The primary thing to keep in mind is that risk is NOT necessarily bad! From a young age, most of us are trained to minimize risk. "No running, wear your helmet, don't do that – it's not safe" were probably all things that we heard as kids. When it comes to personal safety, reducing risk is good. But, taking on calculated financial risk is usually necessary to gain rewards.

We know the old adage: "Higher risk equals higher reward?" As you will learn in this book, this is exactly how the stock market works.

Think of investments as one big spinning roulette wheel (the kind that you'd would find in Vegas). The payout if you place a bet on double-zero is much higher than if you place a bet on red (35-to-1 vs. 1-to-1 odds). Likewise, the odds of hitting a double-zero are much lower than the odds of hitting a red. With roulette, the house has an edge of a little more than 5%. This means that if you play roulette long enough, you will eventually lose all of your money because the house will always win over the long run.

What are the long term odds of investing in the stock market? Would you be surprised to find that the odds are actually stacked in your favor? Unlike gambling, if you invest intelligently in the stock market long enough, the historical odds indicated that you will come out way ahead. *What do I mean about "intelligently" investing in the stock market?* This entire book is focused around addressing that very issue. In particular, Chapter 5 will cover the most important aspects of investing intelligently. For now, let's go back to our roulette example.

Let's say you are in are Vegas, knocking back the drinks and having the time of your life. You just placed a sizeable bet on double-zero and won! Congratulations – how lucky! Now, what if you decided to bet continuously only on the double-zero (high risk bet)? What do you think would happen? You would most likely run out of money after only two or three more spins.

In Figure 1.3.1 below, the historical average return for different types of investments is presented. This represents annual historical returns from the period of 1926 – 2005. These investments are ranked from lowest average return to highest average return. What does Figure 1.3.1 indicate?

Series	Geometric Average	Standard Deviation
Inflation	3.0%	4.3%
U.S. Treasury Bills	3.7%	3.2%
Long-term Government Bonds	5.3%	5.6%
Long-term Corporate Bonds	5.9%	8.6%
Large Company Stocks	10.3%	20.1%
Small Company Stocks	12.6%	32.8%

Figure 1.3.1 – Average Rates of Return for Various Investments

If you are particularly observant you will see that as the average rate of return increases, the standard deviation also increases. *Why is this so important for us to understand?*

It works very much the same way when investing in the stock market. If you put "all of your eggs in one basket," you stand a very high chance underperforming the majority of investors. Sure, there is that chance that you may strike it rich with a couple of lucky bets just like that roulette wheel double-zero bet; but, over the long run you're much more likely to lose most of your money if you focus on extremely high-risk bets.

Without getting too complicated, the standard deviation is basically a measure of the variability in a process (in our case annual stock returns). Higher standard deviation numbers mean that the annual return for an investment is hard to predict and could bounce all over the place. If an investment return is hard to predict year to year, it is said to be more risky.

Figure 1.3.1 tells us that higher risk investments will carry a higher average return over the long run. Why is this the case? Because investors demand a higher potential payout as their investments become more risky.

Let's go back to our roulette wheel example – would people ever place a bet on double zero if the payout were only 2 to 1? Of course not!! Burn this concept into your memory. It is **the** most important concepts in all of investing: **higher risk is necessary for the potential of higher return**.

As mentioned earlier, the standard deviation is a number that describes how variable the likely outcome return can be for each year. Larger numbers mean that you could win big, or you could lose big year-to-year. Let's take "Small Company Stocks" as an example. Figure 1.3.1 tells us there is a 68% chance (the definition of a standard deviation) that the annual return on investing in small company stocks could be anywhere between plus or minus 32.8%. It is great if you happen to have a +33% year, but it isn't so fun if you have a -33% return year. However, over the 80 year period on which the figure is based, you can expect an average annual return of 12.6%!

This works great if you can put your money into small company stocks and not touch it for an extended period of time. The same sort of logic applies to investing in long-term government bonds. The percent swing in annual returns is much lower (only a 5.6% amount for one standard deviation), but you stand to earn a whole lot less over time by investing in these much more conservative instruments (only 5.3% annually).

Have you ever heard the advice that you should take higher risk when you're young and then move into low risk investments as you get older? This principle is based on the standard deviation of the annual return. Think about it – why would you invest in something that gave you only a 5.3% annual return when you could get a 12.6% return?

Well, let's say you're 65 and you've saved up a ton of money in your investing account ($1,000,000 just to make the math easy). You've left everything in the most risky "bucket" – small company stocks. Now, the market decides to teach you a lesson and your stocks drop 33%. You just lost more than $300,000! Sure, you may get it back, but you might die before that happens. You are old, remember?

Alternatively, let's say that when you were 60 years old your small company stocks had a great year. At that point, you decided to move almost everything over into long-term government bonds. Now, if things do not go your way, you might lose 6% in one year. This is not that big of a deal because you only took a paper loss of $60,000. You'll probably have time to make that smaller amount back over time. In this way, you will not be adversely affected by a market downturn at the very time you want to retire.

The same idea also works in reverse. If you are young (let's say in your teens, twenties, or early thirties), then the best place for you to invest is in high risk assets like small company stocks. If you have a couple of bad years (like in 2008 – 2009), that is OK. You have 20-40 years to make it all back. Remember, the long term rate of return is ~12.6%.

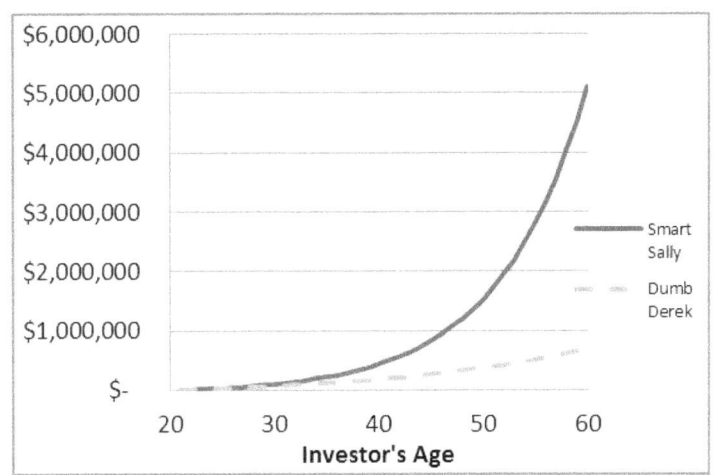

Figure 1.3.2 – Investment Account Value at Various Ages
*Smart Sally invests in Small Company Stock with 12.6%
annual return
Dumb Derek invests in Long-Term Government Bonds at
5.3% annual return*

Figure 1.3.2 is an over-simplification, but it
illustrates the point made above. Let's say we have two
people – Smart Sally and Dumb Derek (again, no relation).
They are both 20 years old, and they are both careful
savers. Both are able to put aside $5,000 a year to invest.
Smart Sally has read this book, and she knows the long
term rate of return for investing in small company stocks
far outweighs more conservative investments. Dumb
Derek decided not to read this book even after all of the
praise and acclaim it has received. Dumb Derek heard all
of the stories about how people lost wheel barrels full of
money in the dot-com crash and the 2008 financial crisis.
He decides to just invest in the safe bet – long-term
government bonds. Just look at what happens.

At age 60, Smart Sally has a retirement fund of
more than $5,000,000 dollars. Dumb Derek's retirement

account only has a value of less than $700,000. Now obviously, there will be many ups and downs with their investments over time. This is not shown in the above figure just for simplicity and understanding. Also, you would be pretty crazy to have 100% of your portfolio in small company stocks as you near retirement age. The smart thing would be to slowly convert you investments over to more conservative assets as you get older. However, I hope you can see that taking an educated approach by accepting calculated risk can really be to your advantage when it comes investing in the stock market – especially when you are young!

We will discuss in more detail, in later chapters, how you can take these types of "smart" risks in the stock market. There are methods that you can easily employ to increase your annual investment returns without increasing your risk substantially. You can even employ some easy methods to increase returns by actually taking on less risk!

1.4 - More Options Equals More Flexibility

What you ever stopped to ask this question: what do I really want most out of life? Most of us get so busy with our day-to-day routines that we often do not take time out to plan where we want to be five, ten, or twenty years from now.

Now, back to the question of what you really want out of life. I bet I can guess your answer, and I have not even met you! Here is my guess: All of us want to spend more time doing the things we love and less time on doing the things we do not love. Is my guess correct?

I have never met anyone who wanted to spend more time raking leaves, cutting the grass, washing clothes, or working in a job they hate just because the pay is pretty good... Time is our most precious asset. Once it is gone you cannot get it back. *How can investing help us to achieve the goal of spending more time doing the things we love?*

Look at it this way: Investing is simply a tradeoff – give up a little bit today to get significantly larger rewards down the road. Would you give up $100 today if it meant 40 years from now I'd give you back that same $100? Of course not! No one would take that deal. What if you could give up $100 today to get back $500 in 40 years? Would you agree to that deal?

Now, what if you gave up $100 today and got back $4,500 in 40 years? I have a feeling most folks would take that deal as long as our basic needs of food, shelter, and clothing were being met currently! The whole point of investing is the concept of delayed gratification. The way compound interest works, the more disciplined one is at putting money aside and not touching it, the bigger your reward will be at the end of the "investing rainbow."

Sure, maybe the flashy among us who are weekend drivers will buy that $80K sports car. With easy financing when we were in our twenties or thirties, just about any type of purchase is possible. However, if we are willing to forgo these types of luxuries and invest the $80,000 instead at an 11% rate of return, over the course of 40 years we would have over $5,200,000! If we assume inflation remains at 3%, you'd be able to purchase 20 sports cars with that amount of money when you hit your sixties!

The main criticism I hear for investing is that you should enjoy your money while you have it. "You never know when you're going to go," is the most argument argument I hear over and over again.

This is true - none of us know when our lives will end; however, you are much more likely to live until you are old. If you fail to invest and plan for your retirement, you may find yourself working as a greeter at a big box store. Is this really the future you want for your sunset years?

Investing while you're young and forgoing certain luxuries means that you'll have more money in the bank as you age. This gives you more options on what direction you want your life to take. Consider just some of the options available to you if you become an intelligent, disciplined stock market investor versus a spend-thrift:

- early retirement
- fund a your children's education
- travel the world on sabbatical
- take a career change or go back to school
- start and fund your own business

The point of this section is to illustrate that having more money gives you more options. Having more options increases the flexibility you have to take control of your life and live it the way you want.

Learning how to invest in the stock market can be the key to winning back your precious time as your wealth begins to grow over the years. Having more wealth means that you will be more able to spend time on the things you love and less on the things you do not absolutely love!

1.5 – Times Are Changing

If section 1.4 of this book did not persuade you that it is time to start saving for your retirement, then let me try a different approach. I will try to scare you into action with doom and gloom. There are four main reasons why you need to get off your butt and start saving and investing for retirement yesterday!

Social Security may not be around when it comes time for you to retire. If it is around, the benefits of this program may be greatly reduced. We have probably all heard this before, but never really sat down to understand fully the impact this would have on us. Not having an extra $1,000 or $2,000 a month in income means that you will have to save and invest a whole lot more over your working career to make up that difference. Simply put, planning that Social Security will help save the day for you when you hit retirement age is a foolish assumption.

Forty or fifty years ago it was common for large companies to offer a defined pension benefit for their employees. Not so much anymore! Almost all companies are going the route of the 401(k) to reduce their management headaches. This means that if you do not get with the program, you will be left high and dry when your golden years approach. If you were promised a pension when you signed on with your company, guess what? There is nothing that prevents them from changing the rules "mid-game" and phasing it out. If you are counting on a pension to save the day, you had better reconsider.

Many that had retired in the past have been able to use their home equity to help make ends meet. They would either take a big payment when they downsized their house, or they would take out a home equity line of credit. This method worked well when property values were increasing 10%-20% a year, but with the recent housing crisis of 2008 this plan backfired on many folks who were ready to retire. There is no way for us to know how housing prices will change in the next 5 – 40 years, but as we will learn later in this book, "putting all of your eggs in one basket" is rarely a good decision when it comes to retirement planning.

If you are planning to save down the road, you may find that there is not a job for you when you reach that older age. It is hard to save for retirement when you are not employed! As jobs in the US become more and more technical and specialized, today's skills may not be marketable in the future as technology can shift rapidly. Additionally, companies will often find it cheaper to layoff senior employees and hire junior folks to perform the same job at half the cost. If you do not have retirement savings in place and this type of event occurs, you will be up the creek!

There are many other reasons why you should be saving for retirement already, but I have covered the most important ones here. Let's move on to Chapter 2 of the book where we will discuss who should invest in the stock market and answer the question: is stock market investing for everyone?

Chapter 2
WHO SHOULD INVEST?

This chapter will answer the question:
Who should invest in the stock market? **We will cover topics such as:**
- **when to get started with investing**
- **401(k)s**
- **IRAs**
- **why it is important to invest even if you have "boatloads" of debt.**

2.1 - The Younger the Better

I am constantly asked the basic question: *when is the best time to start investing in the stock market?* The answer is ridiculously simple - the ideal time to begin investing in the stock market is when you start to earn money as a young adult. For many of us, this could be as early as the age of 15.

Why is investing at a young age so important? There are two main reasons I will share with you. If you read section 1.2 of this book on compound interest, then you already know the first answer! *Hint: the answer rhymes with "hompound kintrest"*…

In addition to compound interest, younger folks can also afford to take substantially more risk with their hard earned money. As highlighted in section 1.3 of this book, the higher risk one takes the greater the potential reward over the long run! This means that when you get to retirement age, you will have a much bigger nest egg if you begin stock market investing early.

To illustrate the power of investing early, let's look at a simple example that compares three different people: Smart Stan, Dumb Derek, and Idiot Isiah. For this example (shown in Figure 2.1.1 below), I have assumed an average annual return that decreases over time as these folks age. Remember, you can afford to take more risk when you are young!

| | | Smart Stan | | Dumb Derek | | Idiot Isiah | |
| | | Annual | Total Account | Annual | Total Account | Annual | Total Account |
Age	Return	Investment	Value	Investment	Value	Investment	Value
15	12%	$ 500	$3,176	$ -	$ -	$ -	$ -
20	12%	$ 2,500	$21,480	$ -	$ -	$ -	$ -
25	10%	$ 10,000	$95,645	$ -	$ -	$ -	$ -
30	10%	$ 15,000	$245,613	$ 15,000	$ 91,577	$ -	$ -
35	9%	$ 17,500	$482,639	$ 23,500	$ 281,542	$ -	$ -
40	9%	$ 20,000	$862,295	$ 32,000	$ 624,699	$ 32,000	$ 191,511
45	8%	$ 22,500	$1,398,992	$ 40,500	$1,155,485	$ 62,000	$ 645,121
50	8%	$ 25,000	$2,202,243	$ 49,000	$1,985,250	$ 91,000	$1,481,756
55	7%	$ 27,500	$3,246,906	$ 57,500	$3,115,083	$ 120,500	$2,768,328
60	7%	$ 30,000	$4,726,475	$ 66,000	$4,748,614	$ 150,000	$4,745,334
65	6%	$ -	$6,325,090	$ -	$6,354,716	$ -	$6,350,327

Invested = $ 852,500 $1,417,500 $2,275,000

Delay Factor =   -   **1.7**   **2.7**

Figure 2.1.1 – Investing at a Young Age

As you can see from the figure above, if Smart Stan starts investing at the ripe age of 15 with $500 a year and follows the same annual contribution plan based on the brackets above, his nest egg could grow to over $6 million by the time he hits 65 years of age. This is based on the returns I have assumed for each age bracket. In total he would have invested about $850,000 in the stock market over those 50 years.

Now, compare with Dumb Derek's example. If he decides to party like it is 1999 until he is 30, how much would he need to invest to end up with the same amount as Smart Stan by the time he hits the ripe age of 65? Well, Dumb Derek would have to invest almost two times as much to hit that goal ($1.4 million vs. $850,000) Delaying those 15 years means that Dumb Derek will need to invest 1.7 times as much money over the shorter period.

In Idiot Isiah's case, if he waits until he is 40 to begin investing, he will need to invest nearly three times as much ($2.3 million vs. $850,000 – a delay factor of 2.7x) to match the performance of Smart Stan! Clearly, if you wait too long to begin investing it is nearly impossible to match the performance of investors who got started at an earlier age. In Idiot Isiah's case, from age 60-65 he would need to be saving $150,000 a year. For most folks, this is impossible!

In all likelihood, the folk who wait to begin investing in the stock market will need to delay their retirement or potentially forgo retirement all together. That is something I hope you can avoid.

Another benefit of learning to invest in the stock market at a young age is that it helps you to develop good financial discipline. If you can develop the beneficial habit of setting aside a certain percentage of income each month for investing in the stock market, then you will train your subconscious mind not to miss that extra money each month. By making the commitment to invest in the stock market, you will learn to reduce all of your expenses.

As your ability to generate income increases over the years, if you remain disciplined with your stock market investing you will be able to contribute an ever increasing amount to your monthly investment (assuming you continue to devote the same percentage of your income to investing). If you commit to sacrificing a little money up front when you are young, you will rise head and shoulders above just about everyone else as you prepare for your golden years. This approach may also give you the option to retire early or take semi-retirement.

Now, let's dive deeper into some of the ways you can begin to invest your hard earned money in the stock market…

2.2 – 401(k)

If the company that you work for has a 401(k) plan, then you should be investing in the stock market! If you run your own business, then you should be investing in the stock market by starting your own 401(k) plan! If your company does not have a 401(k) plan, complain to whomever will listen that you need one right now!

What is a 401(k) plan?

I am glad that you asked! Basically, a 401(k) plan allows you to invest **pre-tax** money in the stock market that can be used for retirement. Typically, companies will match the contribution that you set aside (sometimes even dollar for dollar up to a set percentage). The current annual contribution limit is $17,500 (2014). Your stock market investments will grow tax free until you begin to withdraw the money at retirement age. You can withdraw from your 401(k) at any time, but there is a 10% penalty on any withdrawals made before the age of 59-½.

In the case that you do not realize all of the benefits of this type of retirement savings plan, let me fill you in on why 401(k)s are so great for you and me:

1. 401(k)s reduce your annual taxable income. This means you pay less money to the IRS and keep more for yourself. If you are able to contribute the annual maximum (currently $17,500), you are saving nearly $4,400 a year on taxes! With that kind of extra money, you could buy more than 800 copies of this awesome book to give out to friends and family.

2. Because your money is invested pre-tax, compound interest kicks into high-gear on this untaxed amount that is invested. When you withdraw the money down the road, you'll come out way ahead by using pre-tax money to investment.

3. Most companies have an employer match – this means you are getting free money to invest in the

stock market. Just to make the math simple, say you make $100,000 a year. If you contribute 10% of your income, that's $10,000 a year. If your company matches contributions up to 5%, you are receiving a free $5,000 to invest in the stock market each and every year!

4. If you are self-employed, you can contribute more than $45,000 a year into your own solo-401(k) – all with pre-tax dollars!

5. 401(k)s come with flexibility in how to handle the money if you die and your spouse is still alive. The details are beyond the scope of this book, but there are a number of flexible options your spouse can take to maximize the amount of money that they will receive when they need it.

Now, all of these awesome features that 401(k)s have come with some catches. Be aware of three rules for 401(k)s:

1. When you decide to withdraw the money from a 401(k), you have to pay ordinary income taxes on it.

2. You cannot withdraw the money from a 401(k) until age 59-½ without a incurring a hefty 10% penalty. This is in addition to the ordinary income tax that you would pay outlined in bullet #1 above.

3. When you turn 70-½, you are required to initiate minimum withdrawals from your 401(k) account. The withdrawal rate is designed to reduce your 401(k) to zero prior to your death.

But Derek – what if I have a boatload of consumer debt? Should I still contribute to my 401(k)? Or, should I focus on paying down my debt?

Let's look at a quick example to answer the question you asked. Figure 2.2.1 shows a scenario where Poor Peter has $20,000 of credit card debt. For whatever reason, he cannot transfer his balance and he's stuck paying 12% APR interest on the debt. We'll assume that Poor Peter makes $45,000 a year, and the average stock market investment annual return is 8%.

Year	Debt	Interest Payment		Year	401(k) Savings	Company Match	Investment Value
0	$20,000	$ -		0	$ -	$ -	$ -
1	$18,000	$ 2,400		1	$2,000	$ 2,000	$ 4,321
2	$16,000	$ 2,160		2	$2,000	$ 2,000	$ 8,986
3	$14,000	$ 1,920		3	$2,000	$ 2,000	$ 14,025
4	$12,000	$ 1,680		4	$2,000	$ 2,000	$ 19,467
5	$10,000	$ 1,440		5	$2,000	$ 2,000	$ 25,344
6	$ 8,000	$ 1,200		6	$2,000	$ 2,000	$ 31,692
7	$ 6,000	$ 960		7	$2,000	$ 2,000	$ 38,547
8	$ 4,000	$ 720		8	$2,000	$ 2,000	$ 45,951
9	$ 2,000	$ 480		9	$2,000	$ 2,000	$ 53,947
10	$ -	$ 240		10	$2,000	$ 2,000	$ 62,583

Total Interest = **$13,200**   Total 401(k) Value **$62,583**

Figure 2.2.1 – Debt vs. 401(k) – Cage Match!

What should Poor Peter do in a situation like this?
You may think that since the credit card debt has a higher interest rate than what Poor Peter can get from the stock market (12% vs. 8%), it would be better for Poor Peter to pay off the debt. Let's find out if this is the best strategy.

Let's say that the best Poor Peter can do is save $2,000 a year. This means that it would take him 10 years to pay off all of his debt at 12% APR. At the end of this scenario, Poor Peter would have paid $13,200 in interest. Ouch!

Instead, let's assume that Peter pays the absolute bare amount on his credit card debt (say $20 a month) and invests in his company's 401(k) plan instead. At the end of

34

10 years, Poor Peter has $62,583 in his 401(k)! He could theoretically withdraw all of the money from his 401(k) (this is a horrible idea, but I am just using it for illustrative purposes), pay the 10% early withdrawal penalty on it, pay off the credit card debt, and still be ahead by more than $16,000! Figure 2.2.2 shows the math on this scenario just to illustrate how this would work:

Total 401(k) Value =	$	62,583
Value after 25% Taxes =	$	46,937
Value after 10% Penalty =	$	42,244
401(k) Tax Savings over 10 years =	$	5,000
Total 401(k) Value + tax benefits =	$	**47,244**
Credit Card Balance after 10 years with minimum $20 a month payment =	$	17,600
Interest Payments over 10 years =	$	13,200
Total Money after 10 years of 401(k) =	**$16,444**	

Figure 2.2.2 – 401(k) Wins!

Why would Poor Peter come out so far ahead by contributing to his 401(k) instead of focusing on the credit card debt?

It is because of the company match! Poor Peter would be leaving $2,000 on the table each year by not participating in this company's 401(k)!

In addition, by putting $2,000 into the plan each year, Poor Peter is paying $500 less in federal income taxes each year (assuming he is in the 25% tax bracket) because the 401(k) contributions reduce Poor Peter's taxable income. For this example, the credit card APR on the debt would need to be **nearly 27%** before Poor Peter would be better off to focus on the credit card debt first.

Let me repeat this point just in case you were spacing out for a second. **Unless you have consumer debt**

with APRs > 25%, it is almost always better to contribute to your 401(k) up to your employer match.

One last benefit of the 401(k) that I would like to illustrate is the power of investing with pre-tax money versus post-tax money. Figure 2.2.3 below shows two different investment examples with an 8% annual return. Scenario number one assumes that we have $17,500 a year of pre-tax money to invest. If we use our 401(k) as a pre-tax investment vehicle, the account will grow to $2,141,053 after 30 years (not counting company match).

For scenario number two, what if we decide that the 401(k) is not for us and we invest the money in our own personal investment account. This would be like investing $13,125 each year ($17,500 pre-tax, minus 25% taxes, equals $13,125). At the end of 30 years, our personal investment account will grow to $1,605,790.

Year	Pre-Tax $17,500 Annually	Post-Tax $13,125 Annually
0	$ -	$ -
1	$ 18,900	$ 14,175
2	$ 39,312	$ 29,484
...		
28	$ 1,801,904	$ 1,351,428
29	$ 1,964,956	$ 1,473,717
30	$ 2,141,053	$ 1,605,790

Tax Rate of Withdrawl =	25%	15%
TOTAL After Tax =	**$1,605,790**	**$ 1,364,921**
Pre-Tax Benefit =	**17.6%**	

Figure 2.2.3 – Pre-Tax versus Post-Tax

As you can see in Figure 2.2.3 above, I have made assumptions around the tax rate at withdrawal. For scenario number one, the pre-tax investments will count as normal income and will be subject to a 25% income tax rate. Under scenario number two, we already paid taxes on the money before the investments were purchased, so we will be subject to the lower 15% long term capital gains tax rate.

Because of the power of compound interest, the pre-tax account actually grew to be nearly 18% larger than the post-tax personal investment account. This is the incredible power of using pre-tax investment money. This is why the 401(k) is such an awesome vehicle for building wealth by investing in the stock market!

Now that we have probed the depths of the 401(k) plan, I hope you will agree that you would be brain-dead not to contribute to your 401(k) at least up to your employer match. If you are not doing this, then you are leaving huge overflowing bags of freshly minted money on the table! If your company does not currently offer a 401(k), then put down this book and contact your HR department immediately. I will be waiting here for you to take care of that...

Now that you are contributing to your 401(k) up to your employer match, let's move onto the next best thing for stock market investing - the IRA.

2.3 – IRAs (Traditional and Roth)

Tax advantaged retirement accounts are almost always better than just investing your money in your own personal investment account. This is because you are getting a large bonus by avoiding the payment of taxes at some point in the process – either before your money is invested or at withdrawal of your money. This section of the book will discuss IRAs and how they can be a great tool to help you save for retirement. *What is an IRA?*

Individual Retirement Accounts (IRAs) are another type of retirement account that share some similarities with the 401(k) plan. These programs let you invest in the stock market to save for your retirement. There are many types of IRAs, and some of the more elaborate versions are outside the scope of this stock market investing for newbie's book. The two main types of IRAs that are the most used are the **Traditional IRA** and the **Roth IRA**.

Because Traditional IRAs and Roth IRAs are similar to 401(k) plans and each other in concept, a table that compares the similarities and differences will be the most helpful way for me to show you how each one works. Each of these types of retirement accounts has just enough of a difference between them to make things a bit confusing if not compared side-by-side. Figure 2.3.1 below illustrates the similarities and differences among a 401(k), Traditional IRA, Roth IRA, and a personal investment account.

	401(k)	Trad. IRA	Roth IRA	Personal Investment Account
Max. Annual Contribution	$17,500	$5,500	$5,500	N/A
50 and Above Max. Contrib.	$23,000	$6,500	$6,500	N/A
Contribution Tax Type	Pre-Tax	Pre-Tax	Post-Tax	Post-Tax
Single Income Cap	N/A	$59,000	$112,000	N/A
Married Income Cap	N/A	$95,000	$178,000	N/A
Contribution age	N/A	< 70-½	N/A	N/A
Tax at Withdrawl?	Yes	Yes	No	Yes
Mandatory Withdrawl Age	70-½	70-½	N/A	N/A
Early Withdrawl Penalty	10%	10%	No penalty on Contributions - 10% penalty on earnings	N/A
Withdrawl Age	59-½	59-½	59-½	Any time
Convertible to Roth IRA?	Yes	Yes	-	No
Good for Emergencies	No	No	Yes	Yes
Passed onto heirs	Yes - Taxes due	Yes - Taxes due	Yes	Yes

Figure 2.3.1 – IRA Comparison Table
All values are based on 2014 guidelines

If you are ready to begin investing in an IRA because of its great income tax benefits, you need to make sure you pick the type that is right for you. As you can see from Figure 2.3.1 above, there are several important differences to be aware of between these two different types of IRAs. Generally, investors prefer to use pre-tax money whenever possible because it grows at a faster rate due to compounding (we learned this in section 2.2 of this book). When tax is eventually taken out at withdrawal, you will end up farther ahead by using pre-tax investments.

One problem with IRAs is the maximum income caps on traditional IRAs and Roth IRAs. *How do the income caps affect you and indicate investment programs available to you?*

The income cap values shown in the figure above are established for 2014, and these values will generally increase each year. If you are on the borderline, it will pay to double check your status.

If you do not qualify for a traditional IRA because your income is over the cap, that is OK. You may still qualify for a Roth IRA. A Roth IRA forces you to use after-tax money to invest, but when you eventually withdraw the money at retirement age you will not have to pay any income tax on the earnings. That's right – no tax!

One other great feature of a Roth IRA is that if you need to withdraw some money for an emergency, you can withdraw your contributions (not earnings) without any type of penalty. The same cannot be said for the 401(k) or the traditional IRA – these retirement accounts will hit you with a 10% penalty in addition to the income tax you will be required to pay on the total withdrawal!

I love this feature of the Roth IRA. Because you can withdraw your contributions without penalty, you can almost treat your Roth IRA as an emergency fund. Obviously, you do not want to tap into this money often (if at all). But, it provides extra sense of security if something serious does happen. The option exists to access your finds without paying a huge tax penalty.

2.4 – Everyone!

This chapter was intentionally placed towards the beginning of this book to help you realize that everyone should be saving for their retirement. By investing some amount of your annual income in the stock market, you open more financial options for yourself. If you do not develop the habit of investing periodically at a young age, you will be missing out on hundreds of thousands (or perhaps millions) of dollars to provide for a secure retirement.

If you have not started saving for your retirement yet through investing, do not panic. It is never too late to get started! As the famous Chinese philosopher Laozi once said: "a journey of a thousand miles begins with a single step." Make the commitment to yourself to enroll in your company's 401(k), set up an IRA, or sign-up for your own personal investment account today.

Even if you are tens of thousands of dollars in debt, you should still be investing for your retirement! That's right - company matching and tax incentives will far outweigh the interest you will pay on just about any type of consumer debt. Section 2.2 illustrated how you will be better off in the long run if your first priority is saving for your retirement through a 401(k) versus paying off consumer debt. Unless you have a bounty on your head from a loan shark, or some other sketchy character, investing for retirement should be your top financial priority.

The different types of investments accounts available to you can be a little confusing at first glance. Section 2.3 illustrated the differences and similarities between a: 401(k), traditional IRA, Roth IRA, and personal investment account. Make a mental note of which type or types of investment accounts seems best for you. There will be more discussion in later chapters concerning how you can go about deciding which accounts to put your money in first if you are just getting started with investing.

Now that you are convinced that everyone should be investing in the stock market, we are ready to start funding our investment accounts, right?

Not so fast! First, I want to give you a little more background on the stock market. Chapter-3 will cover: what exactly a **stock** is, what a **bond** is, a brief history of the **stock market**, and how the stock markets of today work.

Chapter 3
WHAT ARE STOCKS, BONDS, AND THE MARKETS?

This chapter will cover the basics of the stock markets. You will learn the difference between a stock and a bond. We will also cover mutual funds, ETFs, the history of the stock market, and how today's stock market works. Finally, we will dive into the details of the different stock purchase orders. You will want to ensure you fully understand this section as the concepts covered here are fundamental to stock market investing.

3.1 – Stock Basics

What exactly is a stock?

I'm glad you asked – let's dig in and find out! If you hunt online, some of the definitions for "stock" are difficult to understand. I will explain what a stock is by using a hypothetical example.

Let's say you are living in the mid 1800's and you are interested in starting up your own buggy whip manufacturing business. There are four basic options available to you to get your company the funding it needs:

1. Have a rich uncle.
2. Use your own money to startup operations.
3. Take out a loan from the bank or other creditors.
4. Find partners that are willing to invest in your business venture by selling them a stake in your business.

If you come from a wealthy family, then choice #1 or #2 may be a viable option for you to get your enterprise off the ground. In this hypothetical case, you are not rich –

sorry! Now, let's move onto option #3 and explore this possibility. You could take out a loan from the bank if you are able to persuade the bankers that you are not a credit risk. Bad news again - in this hypothetical case, you cannot find a bank that is willing to take the risk and lend you the money – dangnabbit! It seems that the only option that will work for your potential buggy whip company is option is #3.

So, option #4 it is! Now let's say you decide to take your yet uncreated company and split it up into 1,000 small little pieces. We call these 1,000 pieces shares of stock (equity). If you are able to persuade your friends, family, and other investors to buy a share of stock, they will now **own** a small piece of your new company. We call these owners of some of the equity in your new company "stockholders." These stockholders are small owners of the company.

Why would anyone want to purchase equity shares of stock in your company?

Well, let's suppose that your buggy whip manufacturing company is wildly successful. Congratulations – I always knew you were destined for success! The buggy whip manufacturing firm can take three actions with its profits:

1. Sell off all or part of the company (assets) and return the money to the owners (shareholders)
2. Reinvest the money to expand business and increase revenues (purchase assets)
3. Pay out the profits to owners (stockholders) and continue operations.

Of course, every company can undertake any number of combinations of these three actions. In this case, because things are going so well, the business will plan to reinvest half of the profits to expand operations. The buggy whip business will take the other half of the profits and distribute them out to stock shareholders (owners).

This payment to shareholders is known as a **dividend**. Out of the total pot of money allocated for a dividend, each shareholder will receive a dividend payment in proportion to the amount of stock they own out of the total amount of stock issued. In this case, after reinvestment in the company, let us assume that there were profits of $500,000 that will be paid out as a dividend to shareholders. Because there were 1,000 shares of company stock issued and sold to investors, each investor will receive $500 per stock share that they purchased.

Why do investors purchase shares of stock in the first place?

All investors purchase a company's stock with the expectations that eventually they will be compensated. These investors are taking a risk by purchasing company shares in the hope that the company will eventually generate a profit. If profits are continually generated, eventually there will be a dividend once the company grows to its desired size.

All long-term investors are ultimately after a dividend. Long-term investors base the amount of money they are willing to pay for a stock on an estimate of how much money the company will eventually earn and pay out as a dividend. I will cover concepts behind this method of stock valuation in greater detail in Chapter-5.

In the example above, I discussed the stock of a single company – the buggy whip manufacturing company. You can see that if investors are working to limit their investment risk, they understand the wisdom of investing in 25 or 30 companies. If investors had most of their money in just two or three companies, any one company could go bust causing them to lose a substantial portion of their investment.

Historically, investors motivated to purchase stock in many companies (25-30 or more) had to pay large fees known as trading commission. Brokers loved this, but as far as the investors were concerned – not so much... If only there were "stocks" that combined the stock of several companies into a single investment. If such a thing existed, then this "bucket" of stocks would certainly make things easier for us. There would be no need to purchase and track 25 or 30 separate stocks concurrently...

3.2 – Mutual Funds and ETFs

For the current day investor – your prayers have been answered! Investment vehicles exist that "bucket" stocks to reduce your commissions and make it easier to keep track of all your investments. The answer to our prayers come in the form of mutual funds and ETFs! *What is a mutual fund?*

That's OK – let me fill you in. A mutual fund is an investment product which pools several different stocks (and potentially bonds) into one package. This makes your life, as an investor, so much easier. These mutual funds are usually managed by the mutual fund manager/team. You can only trade into and out of a mutual fund once per day. Once the mutual fund price "settles" at the end of the day, orders placed by investors to buy or sell mutual funds are executed. Mutual funds can be a great way to simplify your investment portfolio.

All of this convenience comes at a price – mutual funds typically have fees associated with them to compensate the mutual fund manager/team for their work and expertise. These fees are also in place to prevent excessive turnover in the funds (day trading). Annually, these mutual funds expenses can range anywhere from 0.1% to 2.5% or higher! It is extremely important when selecting and investing in mutual funds to pay particular attention to the **annual expense ratio**. This will help you ensure you are not padding another's wallet.

If only there was some type of investment that offered the convenience of a mutual fund but had much smaller fees…Wish no more – the exchange-traded fund (**ETF** for short) offers many of the benefits of a mutual fund minus the high fees. Sure, there are some managing fees, but they are typically only half or one third of their mutual fund brethren. Creating an investor portfolio that uses ETFs is a great way to minimize your investing expenses and maximize your diversification.

The major advantage of ETFs is that they are more tax efficient than mutual funds. Typically, ETFs allow you to delay paying capital gains tax until you actually sell the investment. This is because when you sell an ETF, you are actually selling the physical ETF itself and not the underlying stocks/securities that makeup the ETF. With a mutual fund, the actual individual stocks are bought/sold when a share of the mutual fund is bought/sold. Because of this, a capital gains tax is typically incurred when selling a mutual fund share.

Another minor difference between ETFs and mutual funds is that ETFs are actively traded throughout the day. Remember, mutual funds can only be bought or sold once per day at the close of the market. ETFs can be bought or sold at any time during the day when the stock market is open for trading. This distinction is not very important when you are investing for the long term (not day trading), but it is something that you should understand.

Which is better for your stock market investing- the mutual fund or the ETF? This book will suggest you base your portfolio around investing with ETFs for two main reasons:

1. Because ETF annual expenses are generally half to a third of a mutual fund's expenses, the value of your portfolio will come out much farther ahead over the long run. Would you rather earn an annual 8% return or a 7% return?
2. Because ETFs are more tax efficient than mutual funds, your investments will benefit from higher returns over the long run.

Figure 3.2.1 below illustrates how the two additional annual expenses that typically come with mutual funds (increased management fees and tax inefficiencies) will diminish the value of your portfolio over a 40 year

investment period. For the comparison shown in Figure
3.2.1, assume that you are investing in an S&P-500 type of
index fund. For the ETF portfolio, we will assume an 8%
annual return after expenses. For the mutual fund, we will
assume a 7% annual return after expenses. Also assume
you invest $10,000 a year for 40 years.

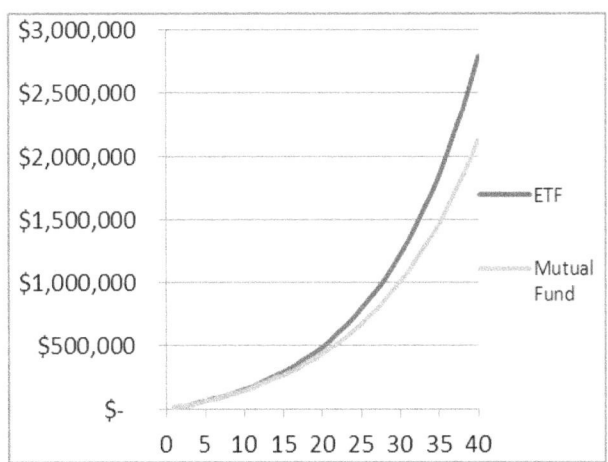

Figure 3.2.1 – ETF vs. Mutual Fund Returns
*Higher Fees and Tax Inefficiencies Impact Long-Term
Performance of Mutual Funds*

As you can see from Figure 3.2.1, if you invested in
a mutual fund that tracked the S&P-500, you would come
out more than $660,000 behind the ETF version of the
same index fund. That amount would surely be enough to
fund years of additional retirement. *Would you rather have
that extra money, or would you rather give it away to your
favorite mutual fund manager?*

Aspect	Mutual Fund	ETF
Fees	Generally higher	Generally lower
Taxes	Inefficient	Efficient
When to trade?	End of Day	Throughout Day
Easily tranferable?	No	Yes
Transparency of holdings?	Daily disclosure	Quarterly disclosure
Commissions	Not usually	Yes

Figure 3.2.2 – ETF vs. Mutual Funds – A Comparison

For your reference, Figure 3.2.2 compares the similarities and differences of mutual funds and ETFs at a basic level. When you are ready to select the types of funds to invest in, I highly encourage you to take a look at the fees to ensure you are not being taken to the cleaners!

3.3 – Bond Basics

This is a stock market investing book – why are we talking about bonds?

Through the advent of mutual funds and ETFs (discussed in section 3.2 above), one can easily invest in these types of instruments as well. In fact, bond investment plays a very important role in nearly every investment portfolio. *What exactly is a bond?*

A bond in its basic form is simply a loan. That is it – there is not much more to it than that! Usually, companies (or governments) will issue bonds to help fund their operations, improvements, or expansions. When you purchase a bond, you are giving the company or government your money up front. This exchange of money comes with the promise you will receive interest on the funds you lend and eventually your initial investment (principal) will be returned to you.

There are many different types of bonds that "tweak" how investors are compensated for the use of their money. Some types of bonds change the amount of interest to be paid, how often the interest is paid, and how the principal will be returned to the investor at the end of the term, etc.

For a basic understanding of investing in bonds through the stock market, there are really only two main factors that you will need to know: the interest rate, and the term.

The interest rate (**coupon**) is the rate that the company (or government) promises to pay at certain fixed intervals. This is defined before the bond is purchased and sold. Bonds can pay interest monthly, semi-annually, or annually. At the end of the term (maturity date), the principal is typically paid back in full to the original investor.

As mentioned earlier, bonds come in hundreds of different shapes and sizes. Terms (maturity) can range anywhere from a one month (e.g.: a one-month US Treasury bill) to 30 years (e.g.: a 30-year US Treasury bond) or longer! Typically, bonds with a term of one year or less are called bills (or T-bills for **Treasury Bills** which have a duration of one year or less). Bonds with a term greater than one year but less than or equal to 10 years are referred to as notes. Bonds with a term (maturity) greater than 10 years are referred to as bonds. Confused with the naming yet? It's OK - you do not really need to know those details other than to impress your friends or family at fancy parties.

Over the long run, bonds have historically given a lower rate of return versus investing in the stock market. Why might this be the case? Most types of bonds carry lower risk to the investor than stocks. Because bonds typically hold a lower risk, the return to investors tends to be lower. Remember that old adage: the higher the risk, the higher the potential return.

There are two main risks that bonds do carry with them: **default risk** and **interest rate risk**. Default risk is the risk that the company, or government, may fail to make an interest payment on time. This would be effectively "short changing" the bond investors. As you can imagine, companies that have a higher default risk, in the eyes of investors, will command a higher amount of interest. This higher interest rate will be necessary to compensate investors for exposure to increased default risk.

Interest rate risk is the risk that bond investors may lock in at a particular interest rate before general borrowing rates begin to rise. The best way for investors to reduce their interest rate risk is to purchase bonds with shorter durations (anything under five years). Another tactic is to buy bonds with different maturity terms as a hedge against rising interest rates. *Have you ever wondered why longer term bonds pay a higher interest rate than short term bonds? Why would this be the case?*

52

As we see with any investment, investments that carry a higher risk will offer investors a higher reward. Investors that purchase long term bonds demand to be compensated for the increase in interest rate risk exposure. This is why long term bonds offer higher interest rate payments.

Because bonds will typically carry much less risk with them than stocks, bonds will have a lower rate of return on investment over the long run. *Because bonds are less risky, do their year-to-year investment returns fluctuate less than stocks?*

Great question! If you refer back to section 1.3 of this book, you will see that the annual fluctuation in bond prices (standard deviation) is also much lower for bonds compared to higher risk stock investments. You can use this interesting fact to our advantage when we go about constructing our portfolio in Chapter 5 of this book. You will come to see in that it is always important to have some portion of your portfolio in bonds.

Why is this so important?

It is important to have some amount of bonds in your because bonds are great at smoothing out the huge drawdowns that can be experienced in your portfolio. If you had a 100% stock portfolio, you could see drawdowns in value up to 90%! Unless you know that you have a "stomach of steel" and can weather the temporary losses in any type of stock market downturn, bonds are a good idea to reduce volatility.

It does not do anyone any good to push risk to the "edge of the cliff" with a 100% stock portfolio only to sell out all of your stocks in a panic. If you do panic in the middle of a down (bear) market and sell your stocks, you will incur significant losses to your principal. Because most people cannot stomach extreme temporary losses that can come with a 100% stock portfolio, most investment professionals recommend a portfolio contain at least a 20%

portion in bonds. We will discuss portfolio asset allocation in much more detail in Chapter 5. This will help you decide what percentage of bonds is right for your portfolio.

3.4 – Brief History of the Stock Market

This section will cover a brief history of the three major US stock market exchanges. This section will give you a little more background on the history of how stock markets work (if you are interested).

The three main stock markets in the US are the New York Stock Exchange (NYSE), the National Association of Securities Dealers Automated Quotation Systems (NASDAQ), and the American Stock Exchange (Amex).

The US stock market came into existence on May 17, 1792 when 24 brokers signed an agreement at 58 Wall Street to buy and sell shares of companies among themselves. The exchange came into existence on March 8, 1817 when the brokers adopted a constitution and named the new entity the New York Stock and Exchange Board.

These brokers actually traded stocks in the out-of-doors from 1817 through 1860 until things were moved indoors. The NYSE still executes a small portion of its trades using the open outcry method - stocks are bought and sold in a process very similar to a live auction. This is becoming more and more outdated as computers take over the matching up buyers and sellers. In fact, the NYSE is the last large stock exchange to use the open outcry trading. Most stock exchanges conduct 100% of their business by electronic trading.

In 1971, the NASDAQ exchange became the world's first electronic trading stock market exchange. This stock exchange was setup by the National Association of Stock Brokers after a **Securities and Exchange Commission** (SEC) report called for improved trading of smaller and less mainstream stocks. The NASDAQ stock market exchange specializes in trading smaller firms that are not yet large enough to qualify for trading on the NYSE. You will find most **initial public offerings** (IPOs) and smaller companies trade on the NASDAQ.

The Amex used to be the "in-between" version of the NYSE and the NASDAQ. It lists and trades stocks that are not yet big enough to trade on the NYSE, but still have a very large following. In recent times, the NASDAQ has surpassed the AMEX in terms of trading volumes. Trades conducted on the Amex can either be conducted manually on the exchange floor or electronically through their computer order systems.

Wasn't that a fun, brief little trip down memory lane?

Again, you do not really have to be familiar with the above to have great long-term investing success, but your knowledge in this area will likely impress your friends, however briefly.

Now that we have a little historical background on the stock market exchanges, let's build on that to understand exactly how stock markets work today in the 21st century.

3.5 – How Today's Stock Markets Work

Each day, billions of shares of stock are traded between investing institutions and ordinary people like you and me. When you create an order to buy or sell stock through the NYSE, Amex, or NASDAQ, you are actually buying or selling on the secondary market. This means that you are not buying the stock directly from a company (e.g.: Pepsi), but you are purchasing it from another investor or trader. This means that the price and quantity for each stock order needs to be agreed upon by both parties (the buyer and the seller).

Each stock has its own market price that fluctuates throughout the day depending on supply and demand for that particular stock. News, economic indicators, and market emotions can all influence the price of stock and cause it to move higher or lower. This change in price will drive the number of shares that will change hands each day (daily stock trading volume). This section of the book will give you a general background on how the stock markets work.

Just about all ordinary folk (like you and me) use an online discount broker for their stock market accounts. These are companies I am sure you have heard of such as: E-Trade, TD Ameritrade, Scottrade, and the like. These online discount brokers allow you to buy and sell shares of stock through their website or specialized software for $5 - $10 per transaction. These discount brokers are great for the small time investor because they drastically reduce the commission fees you pay by directly cutting out the physical stock broker.

In order to buy or sell a share of stock through your online discount broker, you will need to know its ticker symbol. This is the three, four, or five character symbol that represents the stock shares that you are interested in buying or selling. For example, the **ticker symbol** for Intel is INTC, and the ticker symbol for McDonalds is MCD. If you do not know the ticker symbol for the stock you would like to buy, that is OK. There are dozens of ways to find the ticker symbol that you are looking for.

My favorite method to discover the ticker symbol for stocks that I am interested in analyzing further is to use Google Finance. Simply head over to http://finance.google.com and type in the name of the stock or company for which you need the ticker symbol. As an example for this section, let's say that you are interested in investing in the company Netflix, but you do not know the ticker symbol. If you head over to Google Finance and type Netflix into the search bar, we will see that the ticker symbol for Netflix is "NFLX". It really could not be much simpler.

Now that you know the ticker symbol for Netflix is NFLX, you can purchase some NFLX stock during the half-time of Monday night's game, right? Not so fast! The NYSE, Amex, and NASDAQ are only officially open for stock trading during the normal operating hours of 9:30am – 4:00pm EST. Technically, there is after-hours trading for most stocks, but that is really beyond the scope of a newbies book because buying or selling stock after-hours can be much, much riskier.

So, you will need to wait until Tuesday morning to enter your stock order to buy some Netflix (NFLX) stock.

Now, say you wake up Tuesday morning and hear on the radio during your morning commute that NASDAQ futures are down 0.8% overnight.

What the heck does that even mean, Derek?

I am glad you asked! Here goes nothing! The regular stock markets are only open for trading during the day, but futures markets are open 24 hours a day from Sunday night at 6pm EST all the way through Friday afternoon at 4:30pm. Speculators and day traders gamble in the futures market to try and earn a quick buck. This is achieved primarily through using a huge amount of financial leverage. It is extremely risky and not really for the smart long-term investor. Anyhow, commodities and the stock market indexes themselves are traded and speculated on throughout the week (even while you are sleeping). If you hear that "NASDAQ futures are down 0.8%," this means that speculators have driven the price of the overall NASDAQ futures market down by this percentage in after-hours trading.

Derek, where the heck are you going with all of this?

Bear with me here, I am getting to the point soon. If you are interested in placing an order to purchase $1,000 of Netflix stock, then this hypothetical example will directly impact you.

Usually, the stock you are interested in purchasing will open in tandem with the direction of the futures. The initial price offered at 9:30am EST is called the opening price. If the NASDAQ futures are down 0.8% when the stock market opens, there is a good chance that Netflix stock will also be opening somewhere close to 0.8% lower.

It pays to place a little attention to opening price of a stock because you can be fooled if you are not careful. The opening price of a particular stock can be influenced by the futures markets as well as any other type of unexpected news (either positive or negative). If you got ready to buy your Netflix shares and the price were lower than the day before, you would probably be happy, but we are not always that lucky. Let's look at the alternative.

We will assume that you were expecting your Netflix stock to cost you $200 a share. After all, this was the closing price (final price) on Monday at 4:00pm. Now that you are ready to purchase the shares Tuesday morning, the price should be the same $200 a share, right? Nope!

What if there was exceptionally good news overnight and the stock price jumped up 20% in after-hours trading? If you put in a market order to purchase five shares of NFLX stock at 9:30am the next day (5 shares x $200 a share = $1,000), you may end up paying $240 a share! That's certainly not what you intended! Your order to purchase the stock may not even go through if you do not have sufficient capital to cover the purchase. A discussion of the different types of stock orders is definitely needed here!

3.6 – Types of Stock Market Orders

There are two main factors to keep in mind when you are placing an order to buy or sell stock: *price* and *timing*. You can try to guarantee one or the other for yourself, but you can never guarantee both! Do me a favor and re-read that previous sentence a couple of times. When your stock order is executed (filled), you do not want to be surprised with the results.

This section will help you understand all of the different types of stock orders than can be placed so you do not get caught by surprise. I have made mistakes with stock market orders before, and trust me, it is NOT fun! My goal is to teach you the basics here so that you do not make similar mistakes. This topic can be a little difficult to wrap your head around, but it is very important for you to have a basic understanding of the different stock order types.

The first, and most basic, type of order we will discuss is the **market order**. This is the equivalent of saying: *I want to buy or sell this stock right now, and I do not care what the price is!* This type of order will virtually guarantee that you buy or sell the stock, but the price at which the transaction goes through could be unfavorable. Folks entering a market order typically do not mind if they get a sub-optimal price (fill); they want their stock and they want it now. You can see from our Netflix example above (section 3.5) that this has the potential to cause a bit of pain if you are not careful. A market order guarantees *execution*, but not *price*.

How do you avoid paying too much (or selling too low) when buying or selling stocks? If you are looking to conduct a transaction at a very specific, then you will want to use the **limit order**. A buy limit order will guarantee you will not pay more than your set price if you are buying a stock. Similarly, a sell limit order will guarantee you will not sell for a penny less than your set price. Of course the problem is that there may not be someone on the other side of the trade to buy or sell at the price you have stipulated. As a result, your limit order may never get executed (filled). This is why we say a limit order guarantees price, but not execution.

What if you own a stock and you decide you want to limit your risk? You are interested in setting a price to sell the stock automatically if its price begins to drop. You need use the **stop order** to achieve this. A stop order will place a market order to sell the stock if the price "touches" the stop price that you have entered. This type of order is used to help limit your risk. It can also cause you to sell a stock at an unintended price. Because a stop order changes into a market order once the trigger price is hit, you are not really sure what price you will sell your stock. This stop order can help to eliminate some of the emotion involved in stock market investing, but it has its risks. Be sure you consider these risks before using the stop order.

What if you are interested in adjusting up the price of your stop order as a stock you own increases in price each day?

Unless you would like to spend five minutes each day updating all of your stop orders for each and every stock you own, you need to consider the **trailing stop order**. When creating a trailing stop order, you will enter a dollar value per share or percentage decrease at which the stop order will be placed. This means that if a stock continues to increase in value, the stop order price will automatically increase for you. Again, because a stop order is a market order, you need to consider that the stock may sell at a price you were not intending if prices move quickly.

If you like the protection that a stop order gives, but you would also like to guarantee you sell your stock for at least a set amount, then you use the **stop limit order**. This is a specialized order that triggers when a stock price dips below the amount you entered. If the price does dip to your trigger amount, then a limit order will be created to attempt to sell the stock at or above the price you entered. This sounds well and good, but if the price of the stock continues to drop you may not be able to sell your stock with this type of order. Again, a stop limit order guarantees your price. It does not guarantee execution.

There are other more exotic types of stock market orders, but they are beyond the scope of this investing for newbies book. The types of orders covered here will work for you 100% of the time if you are investing for the long term. In fact, the main order type that I propose you use is the limit order. Because you are not day trading, many of these other exotic types of stock orders are irrelevant.

Now that we have discussed the stock market order types, let's cover what length of time stock market orders can remain in effect. **Time in force** (TIF) is the term used to describe how long a stock market order is effective and may be executed. Many market orders to buy or sell stock are entered as **day orders**. This means that they will "expire" at the end of the day they are entered when the market closes. This is usually acceptable for a market order because they are typically executed within seconds of order entry.

Limit orders, where the buy/sell price is set, can be entered either as day orders or **good-till-canceled orders** (GTC). GTC orders typically remain open for weeks to months at a time until either they are filled or your broker removes them. Every broker has a different policy for how long a GTC order may remain active; typically, it is six months or longer. GTC orders work well if you have your mind set on buying or selling a stock at a certain price, but you do not want to sit in front of your computer every day and enter in a new order.

If you are interested in investing in stocks that are not "mainstream" or have lower trading volumes, there is an additional factor that you will need to keep in mind. This is the concept of a **partial fill**. Let's illustrate this point with a simple example. Suppose you want to buy 500 shares of a thinly traded (low volume of shares change hands each day) company's stock. If there are not many people selling at the time you place your order, you may only be able to buy 200 shares at that point in time. At this point, one of two things will happen. The price of the stock will go up and you will purchase more shares at a higher price, or you will just have to wait for another seller to come along. If you would rather have all 500 shares or none at all, then you will need to mark your stock order as **"all or none"** or **"fill-or-kill."**

As you can see, there can be a lot to learn when beginning to invest in the stock market. I hope that this section gives you deeper insight about what stocks really are, how the stock market works, and the different types of stock market orders available to you. If you are feeling a little information overload, don't worry! There were many details in this chapter, but the basic information provided here is really all you need to know to get started investing in the stock market. Learning how to invest in the stock market it just like riding a bike; once you learn, you will never forget.

The next section of this book, Chapter 4, will guide you to the "starting line" of investing in the stock market. Investing in the stock market really is not hard at all with this book as your guide!

Chapter 4
HOW SHOULD I GET STARTED?

This chapter will help you understand how to get started investing in the stock market once you have made the commitment to start investing. We will discuss:

- **financial planners**
- **how you should prioritize your investments**
- **how to determine your eligibility for various investment accounts**
- **how to select an online discount broker**
- **how to setup your first investment account**

4.1 – Go It Alone or Use A Financial Planner?

If you feel yourself saying: *Derek, I am feeling a little overwhelmed at this point* – that is OK. Let's take a little mental timeout and talk about how you can get even more help if you are feeling confused. At this point, we are about half way through the book. If this is all too much for you to keep straight, or you do not think you have the time to manage your investments, you can seek additional support.

There are professionals who can make all of your investing worries go away - financial planners. The downside is that financial planners come at a pretty hefty price! You can literally be forfeiting hundreds of thousands of dollars over a lifetime if you chose to rely on financial planners as a crutch.

Some folks who make the decision to go the financial planner route may find it is the right decision for them. I will try to do my best to persuade you that you can figure out all this stuff for yourself and save a bunch of money in the process. If you feel the temptation to put down this book and make an appointment with your nearest friendly financial planner, I urge you to at least complete this section before you call a financial planner. I think I will be able to change your mind.

Derek, why are you making all this fuss over financial planners?

They are on this earth to help people invest wisely, right? Yes – of course they are. But as you will see, if you follow much of the general advice offered to you in this book, you will likely come out far ahead if you perform your own planning. Why is this the case? I have three words for you (I bet you know them already): fees, fees, fees!

Most financial planners will charge you dearly for their "services." Would you read this book front to back three times if I told you that it would save you $800,000+ over your lifetime? Heck, I would read any book 50 times over if it could make that type of promise!! With that kind of extra money, you could buy more than 175,000 copies of this book to give out freely to every household in your entire hometown/home city!

Most financial planners work by interviewing you, determining how much risk you are able and willing to take, determining your life goals and plans, and then develop an investment portfolio to "sell" you. For this, they will typically charge anywhere from 1% - 2% of the amount you invest annually. Let's take a look at an example to help illustrate the point.

Wise Will purchased this book and decided that he would budget the time to teach himself how to invest in the stock market. Assume he earns a 6% rate of return above inflation. Now, Dumb Derek (no relation) decides that he is too busy to learn the "details" of all of this stock market investing stuff. Dumb Derek hires a financial planner to help him sort everything out. Let's assume that Dumb Derek earns the same 6% above inflation, but Dumb

Derek's financial advisor charges him 1.5% for his services. Dumb Derek is now actually making a 4.5% annual return above inflation.

Assume that Wise Will and Dumb Derek each contribute $10,000 annually from age 20 to age 65 to their retirement account and invest the money in the stock market. Figure 4.1.1 shows the portfolio value for Wise Will and Dumb Derek over the next 40 years. Notice any slight differences?

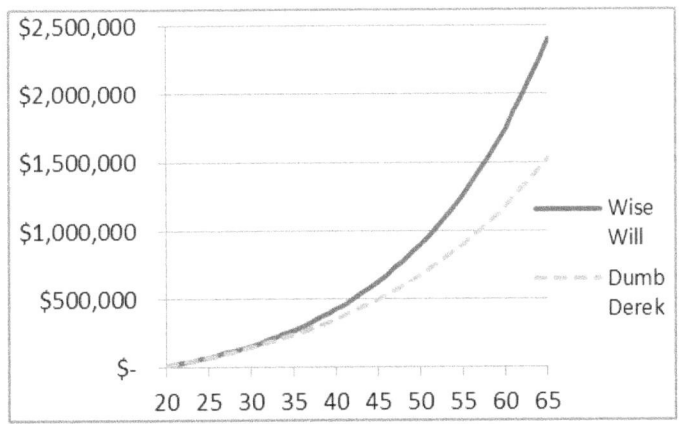

Figure 4.1.1 – Are Financial Planners Helping You or Themselves?

Sure, having a financial planner is a convenience. But is a convenience you can afford? Is it really worth $875,000 to you over the course of the next 40 years? That is how much you will be forfeiting (in today's dollars – remember I used returns above inflation for this example) if you decide to use the services of a financial planner.

I hope you will agree that a couple hours of your time to read this excellent book is worth $875,000 to you. If you are still not convinced that learning about stock market investing is worth your time, then head over to my personal finance blog at www.MoneyAhoy.com and get in contact with me!

4.2 – Investment Priority

Now that you are convinced that you can figure this stock market investing stuff out for yourself, you are ready to start investing in the stock market. Congratulations! You are taking the first steps on the path to achieving your own financial freedom.

*OK Derek, I have made the commitment to begin investing in the stock market – now where should I start? Should I go with a 401(k) first or an IRA? What if I have debt, should I pay that off first or invest first?!? What about an emergency fund?!?!? *Great questions!

Here are my general suggestions for where you should starting investing:

Priority #1: 401(k) up to the company match.

>**Why:** This is the best investment deal for you hands down and should be your first priority. For every dollar you invest, the company also invests one dollar on your behalf. Before any stock, mutual fund, or ETF is purchased, you are already getting a 100% return on your money with the company match. As icing on the cake, using a 401(k) for retirement investing also reduces your annual taxable income! What's not to love here?

Priority #2: Traditional IRA/Roth IRA up to the limit.

>**Why:** This is the second best investment deal for you because of the tax incentives. With a traditional IRA, you'll reduce your annual taxable income (this is like a 25+% return right off the bat). For a Roth IRA, you will pay the income tax up front, but then you will not need to pay taxes when you withdraw your money (this is like a 15% -30% bonus when you withdraw your money at retirement age). You definitely do NOT want to pass up this retirement investment account if you quality. (For

more on IRA qualifications and limitations, see Section 2.3 of this excellent book.)

Priority #3: Pay off consumer debt if > 4% APR.

    Why: If you have started funding your 401(k) up to the company match and funded an IRA up to the allowable limit, now it is time to focus on reducing your consumer debt. It generally makes sense to attack this if your average APR on the debt is greater than 4%. If not, it is generally advised to continue making the minimum payment and move onto priority #4. Consumer debt includes things like car loans, student loans, credit card balances, etc. Other folks might advise paying off debt before investing, but as Section 2.2 demonstrated, you will actually come out farther behind by doing this unless your debt APR is extremely high (> 20+%).

Priority #4: Fund your 401(k) up to the annual limit ($17,500 in 2014)

    Why: The 401(k) investment up to the allowable annual limit still provides valuable benefits. You are reducing your taxable income now and letting your investments compound with pre-tax money. In Section 2.2, we learned that investing with pre-tax money beat post-tax investing hands down. If you can afford to invest all the way up to $17,500 in your 401(k), then great for you!

Priority #5: Create a small emergency fund.

    Why: This one gets a bit tricky depending on whom you ask. Each of us has a different risk tolerance for how much cash we prefer to keep in the bank. Most folks will argue that six months of expenses should be held for emergencies at all times. I am recommending the emergency fund at priority #5 for a couple of reasons.

        First, if you run into a true emergency, you can withdraw the contribution portion from your

Roth IRA without penalty. Also, why build an emergency fund if you have debt? You are just running up the interest "tab." This makes absolutely no sense. It is better to pay off debt (such as credit card balances) aggressively. If an emergency does pop up, your last resort can be to use the credit card. The worst case scenario is that you end up with additional credit card debt to repay. The best case scenario is that you pay off your credit cards early and save hundreds or thousands on interest payments if no emergency occurs! Other folks will argue that having un-invested cash savings is a waste of capital. In the end, this one all comes down to your risk tolerance. I will let you decide what is your risk comfort zone.

Priority #6: Fund a personal/individual investment account.

Why: If you have made it this far and still have money left over to invest, then congratulations! You truly are a master at managing your money. Now is the time to setup a personal/individual investment account and begin to fund it with the money you continue to save each month. If you have made it all the way down to this priority, you will be on your way to financial security! There are no special tax incentives, no interest to avoid, and no emergencies to plan for, which is why this shows up as the last priority when it comes to investing in the stock market. As we learned in Chapter 1, investing your money in a personal investment account for the long-term beats keeping the money in a bank account hands down. When your investments are sold, you will be able to enjoy a lower long-term capital gains tax rate.

Now that you have seen my recommended investment account funding priorities, you can start to formulate a plan of attack that will work best for your personal situation. Once you have your plan developed, we can move into taking your first step towards action and greater financial freedom.

4.3 – Take the First Step

OK Derek, I have developed my plan of attack. Now what?

Let me again congratulate you on taking this huge step forward! You have your plan of attack ready and you know which accounts you like to setup first to begin your stock market investing journey. If your investment priority plan involves funding a Traditional IRA or a Roth IRA, please do yourself a small favor. Quickly re-read section 2.3 to determine the type of IRA for which you are eligible. This will save you some headache down the road – trust me.

Now, this next step is going to sound a little corny, but bear with me here. There have been countless studies that show that we, as humans, do not really like change. We are more comfortable maintaining the status quo. If you are to begin investing, you need to make the personal commitment to get started by creating a goal for yourself to get all your accounts setup in the not too distant future.

Most of these investment accounts will require about two weeks to establish completely. Make the personal commitment to yourself now to get these accounts setup in the next two weeks. It is an administrative pain in the butt, and most folks will put it off. Filling out forms is not the most enjoyable activity in the world. If this sounds like you, then I would suggest posting a reminder or goal on your refrigerator to keep you motivated to go through this one-time setup pain.

One thing that you will want to think about before you setup your investment accounts is how you will fund them. You will need to decide the amount of money you will make available for your initial deposit as well as the amount you will contribute each month. You do not have to have a definite plan for how much you will put in each account or how much you will transfer into each account monthly, but it is generally a good idea to have a rough sense before getting started with the account setup. Some accounts that you set up will give you special treatment if you signup to fund automatically an investment account with a specified amount each month. Other accounts will have a minimum funding level that you will need to meet.

It is now time for the rubber to hit the road. I you have not already done so, create a full mental plan for what type of accounts you would like to setup, commit to the two week timing goal, and decide how much you will place into each investment account. Once you have determined this mentally, write it out and post it on the fridge and force yourself to do it!

Now, all we have to do is pick a broker and start filling out forms. Fun times lay ahead!

4.4 – Picking an Online Brokerage Firm

Your first priority should be setting up your 401(k). (See Section 4.2 if you need a refresher as to why.) There are not many specifics we can discuss here because this process will be handled by your company (unless you are self-employed), and the paperwork to fill out should be relatively straightforward. Setup an appointment to meet with someone in your Human Resources department or the person in charge of administering your 401(k) at your company. If your company does not currently offer a 401(k), then complain like crazy to whomever will listen! Your company needs to offer a 401(k) retirement investing plan today!

Now, with the 401(k) plan under control, let's proceed to how we can setup an investment account to fund priorities #2 and #6 – IRAs and personal/individual investment accounts. Dozens of online brokers are available for your selection. Some online brokers focus more on trading rather than investing. Focus your search on brokerage firms that are good at investing for the long-term versus short-term trading.

Figure 4.4.1 lists five of the most popular online brokerage firms with their associated websites. Each one of these company's websites will try to persuade you why they are better than the others. I am a bit hesitant to include the fees these brokerages charge for a trade because this changes over time. Typically, you can get a rate per trade than what is advertised if you simply call them and request it. I actually get trades for $5/trade with TD Ameritrade versus the advertised $9.99 per trade.

You will notice that the rates these online brokers charge per trade are basically similar. I have used the top three on the list and personally prefer TD Ameritrade because of their charting and software programs. I really disliked the overall experience I personally received when dealing with Scottrade; I have included it in the list because of its popularity. The choice is up to you and there probably will not be much of a difference between any of them in over the long run.

Broker	Website	Trade Rate	IRAs
TD Ameritrade	www.tdameritrade.com	$ 9.99	Yes
ETRADE	www.etrade.com	$ 9.99	Yes
Scottrade	www.Scottrade.com	$ 7.00	Yes
TradeKing	www.tradeking.com	$ 4.95	No
OptionsHouse	www.trademonster.com	$ 4.75	No

Figure 4.4.1 – Online Broker Comparison

One thing I would like you to consider when selecting an online broker is whether they offer IRA accounts in addition to the traditional investment account. It will make it that much easier for you to manage if you can find a broker that will allow you to setup two investment accounts - an IRA account and a personal investing account under the safe "roof." I favor TD Ameritrade because it provides the convenience of having all of my accounts set up with the one company.

One final consideration you should give is the minimum funding amount. If you are starting out with a small amount of money to invest, that is OK. You will want to check the brokerage website you are planning to use to ensure that you have enough money to meet the minimum funding requirements. I have intentionally left this out of the table above because the amount routinely changes.

Once you have decided what brokerage firm you will use, it is time to fill out some paperwork! Most brokerage firms these days will let you fill everything out electronically (including your signature), which is a nice feature. The final section of this chapter will briefly cover what information you will need to have handy to set up one or more investment accounts. It pays to be prepared with all your info before you start to fill out the forms.

4.5 – Setting Up an Account

Now that you have selected your online brokerage firm, let's briefly cover the typical information you will need to have at hand to complete the necessary paperwork. I would plan to spend 20-30 minutes for each account you are creating. Here is the information you will need:

- Your social security number or Individual Taxpayer Identification Number (ITIN)
- Your name, address, phone number, email address
- Date of birth, marital status, mother's maiden name, number of dependents
- Your employer name and address
- Annual income
- Approximate **net worth**
- Approximate **liquid net worth**
- Type of account that you would like to open (Individual, Traditional IRA, Roth IRA)

One thing to keep in mind when filling out the online paperwork is that most online brokerage firms will require you fill out two separate applications if you are creating an IRA and a personal/individual investment account. If you plan to setup both, be sure to schedule at least 45 minutes to complete all the forms.

If you followed all the steps in this chapter, then you will have your 401(k) account setup through your company. Additionally, if you have extra money each month to invest you may have also selected an online broker and setup an IRA and/or personal/individual investment account. Congratulations! Now, let's discuss where we should put (allocate) your money so that you have your risk spread around and you are receiving a good return on our investments.

Chapter 5
WHERE SHOULD I PUT MY MONEY?

Now that your investment accounts are setup and funded, you are ready to jump in with both feet and start investing! This chapter will cover:

- **stock pricing**
- **stock picking**
- **diversification basics**
- **market index funds**
- **asset allocation basics**
- **several asset allocation examples.**

When you master this chapter, you will be on your way to long term investing success!

5.1 – Stock Pricing

Derek, what is the secret formula for helping me to buy stocks at a low price and then later sell them to someone else at a high price?

Well folks, I am sorry to tell you that things are not quite this simple when it comes to investing. This section will demystify why stock A is $10 a share and stock B is $20 a share. This is the first step to understanding the intricacies of stock picking.

Recall from section 3.1 of this fantastic book that the sole reason investors purchase stock is that they expect to get a return on the investment of their money. This return on investment is expected to take the form of dividends paid out to stockholders from the profits the company generates. This is the basis for the current market price of any particular stock.

If investors believe a particular company will be successful and generate enormous profits, they will be willing to pay more for the stock. If investors believe a company will only generate moderate profits, then this stock will not be valued as highly in comparison.

So, a $20 stock is expected to perform better than a $10 stock, right?

Nope, not at all the way it works. If only it were that easy! Because each company has issued a different number of stock shares, if share prices are compared directly on-n-one it would be an apples-to-oranges comparison. There is a way to normalize the prices of the stocks so that you can get a meaningful comparison of stock prices among companies. The most commonly used method for stock pricing comparison is the **price to earnings ratio** (or the P/E ratio – PE for short).

Let's look at a quick example to help you understand how this is done. Assume the price of one share of Home Depot (HD) stock is currently trading for $79 a share. A quick check will reveal that there are 1.41 billion shares of HD stock currently issued and the most recent annual earnings for the company were reported as $5.29 billion. It is possible to calculate earnings per share (EPS) using this process: $5.29 B in earnings divided by 1.41 B shares = $3.75 in earnings per share. Take the current market price of the stock and divide by the EPS – this gives us a P/E ratio of **21.1** ($79 / $3.75 = 21.1).

Great Derek, so we know that the P/E ratio of Home Depot is 21.1 – what does that help us with?

I am so glad that you asked! Let's look at the P/E ratio for a company like Amazon (AMZN). Running through the same calculation, you can see that the current P/E ratio of Amazon is 640!! For the amount of earnings that Amazon is currently generating, investors are willing to pay over 30x compared to Home Depot.

What in the world is going on here?!?!? Clearly someone must have it wrong!

Not necessarily. You see, investors currently believe that Amazon will grow its earnings over the years to justify this seemingly higher price (expressed by the 640 P/E ratio). If investors in Amazon are correct, then the price they paid for the stock is a good investment. If, on the other hand, it becomes clear that Amazon will not be able to continue to grow its profits as aggressively as assumed, then the price of the stock will fall until the P/E ratio comes back down to earth.

In essence, the current price of any stock is the combined collective wisdom (or stupidity) of the millions of investors the world over. Did a company just release a new technology that will revolutionize their industry? If this shifts the collective assumptions around their profit growth, then the stock price will increase to reflect this. Was news just released that confirms that a company is becoming less relevant in the marketplace? This will decrease the collective assumptions around profit growth and cause a company's stock price to decrease. The earnings potential of the buggy whip manufacturing company might not be as bright in 2014 as it was in 1880!

Now that we know a little bit about how and why stocks are priced the way they are, how can we use this to our advantage?

If there were a surefire way to identify precisely when stocks were overpriced or underpriced, it would be possible to develop a reliable method to buy low and sell high. If I knew some kind of secret formula to help me do this, then I would be rich! Let's explore this topic in the next section – stock picking.

5.2 – Stock Picking

Did you know that if you would have bought $100 of Home Depot stock in 1981, it would be worth more than $220,000 today?

If you factor in reinvesting the dividends, you would have well over $400,000!! How is that for picking a great stock?

If only our investing lives could be this simple. The trouble is, we can never know ahead of time which stocks will grow their earnings far in excess of what the majority of investors are expecting. Likewise, we can never know ahead of time which stocks will "flame out" to become the great "has-beens" of the upcoming decade.

If there were a magic formula for picking stocks, then certainly folks would not be very inclined to share this information with others. Think about that for a minute... If someone had discovered a repeatable method to identifying the best returning stocks or trading methods, do you think they would sit down to write a newsletter about it? No! They would be selling everything they owned that was not nailed down so that they could invest and grow rich themselves.

Because no one can accurately predict which companies will perform better than expected and which ones will not, there is little use in trying to join the herd by becoming yet another tea leaf reader. Do you think you are that much better than the millions of other folks that are playing the "stock market trading game?"

By trying to pick the best individual stocks for your own portfolio, you may get lucky and come up with some real winners once in a while. But, it is almost impossible to continue to outsmart the millions of other investors on a consistent basis year-over-year by picking your own individual stocks. As we mentioned in a previous chapter, this is akin to walking over to a roulette table and placing all your money on "33." The payout may be large if you happen to be correct the first time, but you are much more likely to lose a lot of money using this type of approach.

Folks that take on this type of stock market investing approach are quick to point out their winners. Putting "all of your eggs in one basket" can work for a time. But, over the long-run, this type of high-risk strategy is almost certain to end in sub-par performance. And, we certainly do not want sub-par performance for you for you.

To use a basketball analogy, there comes a point in time when all of us need to be practical and go for the easy layup versus shooting that half-court, one-handed shot at the buzzer. Those half court shots are awesome, and they certainly make the news, but they are also a one in a thousand type of event. We need to implement something a little more reliable for ourselves that will not be "shooting for the moon."

5.3 – Diversification Basics

The answer to getting all of your "eggs out of one basket" is diversification. Simply put, diversification means reducing your investment risk by spreading your money around into different asset classes. When it comes to investing, not all investments will move up and down at the same time. Diversification takes advantage of this phenomenon to reduce your overall portfolio risk. By diversifying, you give up the chance for "one-in-a-thousand" type of phenomenal performances. For this sacrifice you are rewarded by lower overall portfolio risk. Just to boil the concept down – you will not win big, but you will not lose big either.

To demonstrate this point, let's use a simple exercise: would you rather have a one in five chance of achieving a 30% return, or an eighty percent chance of receiving a 10% investment return? From Figure 5.3.1 below, we can see that the best choice is actually the more conservative approach.

Likelihood	Potential Return	Predicted Return
20%	30%	6%
80%	10%	8%

Figure 5.3.1 – Diversification Example

This is the power of diversification. Diversification reduces the potential return that we will achieve – this is because we are not going for that half-court, at the buzzer, high-risk, three-point shot. We are aiming for something much more achievable like your run of the mill, two-point layup. Diversification increases the likelihood that you will get a decent return. After all, the chance of making a layup is consistently higher than hitting a half-court shot.

When these factors are combined (multiplying the probability by the potential return) we actually come out ahead in the long-run by taking the more conservative approach. Can you imagine an entire basketball game where one team only scored through layups while the other team only ever tried to hit three-point, half-court shots? While fun to watch, there is no question which team would come out ahead in the long run!

There are several main "buckets" that investors employ to diversify their investment dollars. These are:

- **US Stocks** – or sometimes referred to as domestic stocks. This bucket can be broken down farther into: large value, large growth, small value, and small growth stocks.
- **Foreign Stocks** – these are stocks of companies that mainly exist outside of the US. This bucket can be further broken down into: Europe, Pacific Rim (Japan), and emerging markets (BRIC – Brazil, Russia, India, China).
- **Bonds** – or sometimes referred to as fixed-income securities. This bucket can be further broken down into: treasury bills, treasury notes, treasury bonds, corporate bonds, municipal bonds, and junk bonds, just to name a few.
- **REITs** – this stands for real-estate investment trusts. These are investments that own income producing commercial real-estate and typically pay out hefty dividends that are generated from the rent paid by tenants.

When constructing our own investment portfolios, we should envision that we are seated at an all-you-can-eat buffet with the family. Let's call it "Warren's All-You-Can-Eat Buffet"…(I thought of that one myself). **But, with this restaurant there's just one catch - we only get**

one plate! If we end up loading up our plate with something that tastes horrible, we will just have to sit there in our seats moping around until it is time to leave. Sure, everything looks good at first glance, but looks can be deceiving.

Because we have not been to this restaurant before, and the cook is always experimenting with changing the menu, we are not sure exactly what is good and what we should pass over. So, what does the smart restaurant patron do? She could load up her entire plate with mashed potatoes. That might work just fine for her. But suppose what she thought was mashed potatoes was actually mashed cauliflower? Now what should she have done? (Please don't ask me how I know what mashed cauliflower tastes like!)

Ok, back on topic.

In the analogy above, loading up your portfolio with just one type of stock or asset class is like choosing only mashed potatoes (or what looks like mashed potatoes). You are taking basically an "all-or-nothing" approach with your money. That might work for you, but for me that is taking on an insane amount of risk with your financial future.

Isn't it wiser to fill your plate with a little bit of everything? Diversify what you select into maybe into five or six categories? This way, you are almost certain to find something that you will like and will work for you. If those mashed potatoes turn out to be mashed cauliflower, you will still be OK. You can just enjoy the macaroni and cheese, and that small piece of cheese cake that you also made room for on your plate!

To take this analogy just a bit further, suppose that the buffet has hundreds of different types of foods to choose from. It is not really practical to sample thousands of different foods with only one plate. How can you be reasonably sure that you will get to experience a good cross-section of all the best foods that are offered? In the case of "Warren's All-You-Can-Eat Buffet" you are out of luck. But, in the stock market investing world, you are fortunate to have a different kind of buffet – the market index fund.

5.4 – Market Index Funds

A **market index fund** is a portfolio of assets constructed to match, or track, the components of a market index, say for example the S&P-500. If you attempted to buy all 500 stocks in the S&P-500, you would pay $2,500+ in fees alone! Not to mention, you would need mega-bucks just to afford one share of each of the 500 different stocks that make up this index.

Instead, you can purchase shares of an S&P-500 market index fund. These funds hold all 500 stocks that make up the S&P-500. When you purchase a single market index fund stock share, you are purchasing tiny fractions of each of the S&P-500 stocks. The difference is that you pay only a $5-$10 fee for the entire transaction. Talk about a savings! The market index fund will move up and down in tandem with the S&P-500 minus a very small management fee. These fees are typically as low as 0.2% a year – a fraction of the fees charged by a full-service broker.

If you are still having trouble conceptualizing what a market index fund is, think of it like a super multi-vitamin. Instead of spending huge amounts of money to eat dozens of diet supplements to get all of your essential nutrients, you can simply take one multi-vitamin that has all of the important nutrients in a small, easy to ingest pill. The S&P-500 multi-vitamin market index fund would have all of the 500 most important nutrients that you would need to survive.

Just as there are different types of multi-vitamins you can purchase, there are different types of market index funds and ETFs available for investing. Figure 5.4.1 shows a small sampling of some of the more popular index funds available for investment:

Name	Ticker	Asset Class
Energy	VDE	Energy Stocks
FTSE All-World ex-US	VEU	International
FTSE Developed Markets	VEA	International
FTSE Emerging Markets	VWO	International
FTSE Europe	VGK	International
FTSE Pacific	VPL	International
Health Care	VHT	Health Case Stocks
High Yield Bond ETF	JNK	Bonds-Junk
REIT	VNQ	Real Estate Stocks
Short-Term Bond	BSV	Bonds-Short Term
S&P-500	SPY	S&P-500 Stocks
Small-Cap Value	VBR	Small Cap, Value Stocks
Total Stock Market	VTI	International
Utilities	VPU	Utility Stocks

Figure 5.4.1 – Example of Market Index Funds/ETFs

As you can see, it is possible to own fractions of thousands of different stocks from around the world. The fees charged for this service are typically only 0.1% - 0.3%. These market index funds allow you to diversify your investment dollars effectively without breaking the bank from excessive commission fees. For a complete listing of popular market index funds and ETFs available to you, head over to http://www.spdrs.com or http://www.vanguard.com.

Now that you have a better understanding of the power of market index funds and how they can help you to achieve good diversification for your portfolios, you are almost in the home stretch. Having learned that it is a bad idea to "put all of our eggs in one basket," it is necessary to decide the number of baskets to use. You also need to decide how to shift the number of eggs you put in each basket over your investing lifetime. This leads to the subject of asset allocation.

5.5 – Asset Allocation Basics

In section 1.3 of this book, it was seen that different types of assets have different long term expected rates of return on your investment. This is because some assets are inherently riskier than others. Investors who are willing to take more of a gamble can expect a higher return for their money. Increased risk usually means increased returns over the long run.

The list below arranges investment "baskets" in the order of lowest to highest risk:

1. **Cash** – This is the money you have sitting under the mattress, in your bank account, money market account, or your investment account. Your dollars are backed by the full faith and credit of the US government and the closest thing we have to zero risk.
2. **Bonds** –Section 3.3 of this book states that bonds are debt instruments or IOUs. They come in different maturities varying from one month to 30 years or longer.
3. **Large Cap Stocks** – These are large capitalization stocks. This means that the total size of value of the company is large in relation to all of the companies of the world. Think Wal-Mart, McDonalds, General Electric, Exxon Mobile, etc.
4. **Real Estate** – This is land, residential property, and commercial property. A convenient way to invest in real estate, if you do not want the hassle of dealing with rental units, is through purchasing REIT stocks. REIT stocks were discussed briefly in section 5.3.
5. **International Stocks** – Otherwise known as foreign stocks. These carry higher risk because they usually involve smaller

companies in more volatile markets and in less politically stable countries.

6. **Small Cap Stocks** – These can be the most risky types of stocks. These are small startup companies that are typically listed on the NASDAQ. They offer high potential rewards because of their high risk.

I have given you a general sense of the "riskiness" for different assets and how they compare to each other. Now, let's discuss asset allocation. It would stand to reason that if you are a conservative investor, you would want to stick mostly with the low-risk type of assets. Similarly, if you are an aggressive investor, you'd pick mostly high-risk assets for your investments.

Figure 5.5.1 illustrates three different types of asset allocations. Each different type of asset is shown as a "basket" to hold eggs. Assets with low risk are placed on the left side of the illustration, and assets with high risk are placed at the right side. Notice that the conservative asset allocation has most of the "eggs" in the low risk baskets. The moderate asset allocation has "eggs" in all the baskets, mostly allocated in the middle baskets. Finally, the aggressive asset allocation has "eggs" in mostly the higher risk assets.

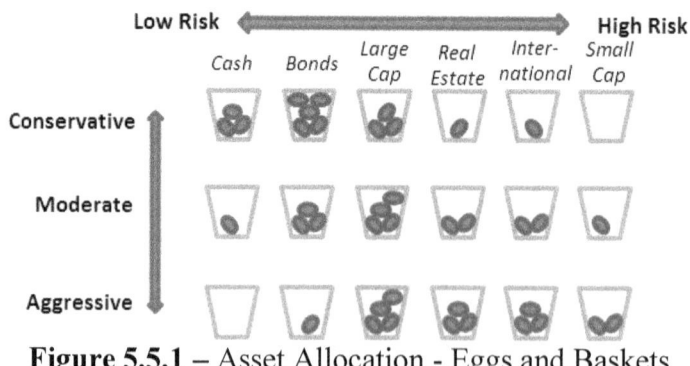

Figure 5.5.1 – Asset Allocation - Eggs and Baskets

Typically, when investors are young they start with an aggressive asset allocation. This is because they can afford to continue investing when downturns in the stock market occur. They will not need the money for a long time, so there is time to recoup any short-term paper losses if a market downturn occurs. As one ages, it is typically suggested to shift to a more moderate asset allocation. This is because one has less time to "win" back losses if a large stock market downturn occurs. As one nears retirement age, it is suggested that one take on a conservative asset allocation. This is because a severe market downturn would dramatically impact one's ability to retire and live comfortably if one is heavily invested in risky assets.

Of course, everyone's situation is different. Some people are able to tolerate a high degree of temporary losses without freaking out and selling all of their stocks during a market downturn. Others are extremely risk averse and hate seeing any type of large investing loss as they save for retirement.

The usual suggestion for those of us who have no stock market experience is to start with a moderate asset allocation. Once you have survived your first stock market downturn (bear market), then you can reassess your risk tolerance and possibly move into more aggressive asset allocations. I wish I had seen this advice when I first starting investing. I could have saved myself thousands of dollars!

Others suggest that young investors go all out and enter aggressive investments from the very start. This is fine if you are extremely disciplined and able to leave your investments alone during a downturn. Many investors think they have the fortitude to withstand a bear market only to discover they sell out near a market bottom. The choice is yours, but I would recommend starting with an initial moderate asset allocation until you get some stock market investing experience under your belt. Once you gain additional experience, you can then adjust your overall portfolio to suit your risk tolerance.

You will notice in Figure 5.5.1 above, I created six different asset "baskets." Some investors get fancier and break the bonds down into multiple durations (6-month, 1 year, 2 year, 5 year, etc.), international into different categories (Europe, Pacific Rim, BRIC,), etc. The number of baskets you decide to use for your portfolio is really up to you. The more baskets you create, the better diversified you will be. The downside to having a lot of baskets is that it will be more difficult to stay organized, and you will probably incur higher transaction costs. For these reasons, I would recommend starting with just these six investment baskets. You can always add baskets later as you gain stock market investing experience if you feel it necessary to branch out.

At this point, I think you have developed a good understanding of eggs and baskets. We are ready for the last section of this chapter. In the final section we will look at a couple different asset allocation examples. If you have been following along so far and understand all of the concepts I have presented, then you are ready to pick an asset allocation from the next section or develop your own!

5.6 – Asset Allocation Examples

With the basics of asset allocation under your belt, you can dig in a bit more and look at some specific asset allocation examples. This section is meant to serve as a guide to help plan some different types of asset allocations that might work for you. When deciding on your specific asset allocation, it all comes down to how much risk you are willing to take. Generally, increased risk means increased returns over the long term.

There is one caveat to this that I would like to point out. I touched on it earlier, but it bears repeating. Targeting your asset allocation to favor higher risk investments does you no good if you panic during the first downturn and liquidate your investments. This will only serve to lock in your losses. Because of this, even the most aggressive asset allocations should not plan to have a 100% allocation of stocks. A good and recent example of this was the severe bear market from 2008 – 2009. Do you think you would be one of the lucky few people that were mentally prepared to withstand the 70% - 80% drop in asset prices that occurred without completely freaking out? If you are not sure, then it is probably not a good idea to go "all-in" with stocks. For this reason, many intelligent investors maintain at least a 20% allocation of their portfolio in bonds.

The normal variations in the stock market are not accidental or avoidable. The system is designed to routinely expand and contract. The consequence is that nervous or over-extended investors are prone to lose a lot of money in the stock market. Frequently, the loss of one investor is the gain of another. Many financial advisors "churn" stock accounts in order to collect transaction fees. These persons make no money when you invest carefully for the long term and refuse to chase after high risk gains like a chicken with its head cut off. Keep this in mind when looking over some of the assets allocations presented here. You are investing for the long term and are not concerned with day-to-day movements!

Figure 5.6.1 below gives several different detailed asset allocation examples. Feel free to use any of these for your own portfolio, or work to create your own. There are literally infinite combinations, and there is no right or wrong answer. Just make sure that the asset allocation choice you make matches up with the amount of risk you are willing to take and your investment time horizon goals.

Risk Profile	Cash	Bonds	Junk Bonds	Large Cap / Total Market	Real Estate	Inter-national	Emerging Market	Small Cap
Conservative	20%	60%		12%	4%	4%		
Moderately Conservative	10%	45%		30%	5%	5%	5%	
Moderate	5%	30%		40%	8%	7%	5%	5%
Moderately Aggressive		15%	10%	35%	13%	13%	7%	7%
Aggressive			20%	30%	15%	15%	10%	10%
Ticker Symbol -->	-	BND	JNK	SPY or VTI	VNQ	VEA	VWO	VBK

Figure 5.6.1 – Asset Allocation Examples

Notice in Figure 5.6.1 above that the least risky assets are listed on the left with the most risky assets listed on the right. As we move from conservative to moderate to aggressive asset allocations, notice how assets on the right hand side begin to increase in percent weight. This is because we are moving money from the more conservative assets into the more aggressive (and thus riskier) assets.

The following figures 5.6.2 – 5.6.6 break down the above table into pie-charts to help you visualize how each of the asset allocation differs:

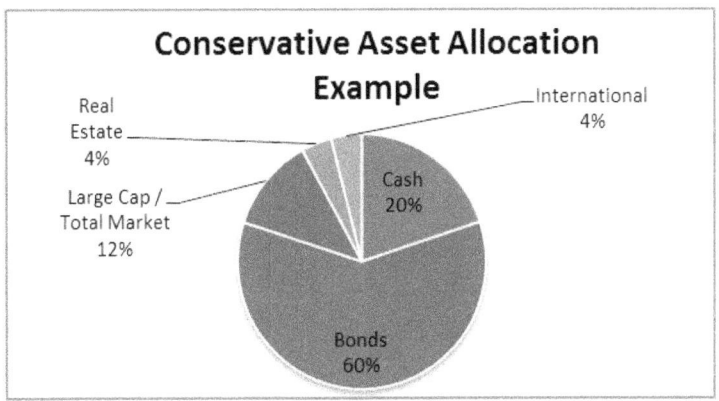

Figure 5.6.2 – A Conservative Asset Allocation Example

For the conservative asset allocation, you can see that a majority of the money is placed in fixed income securities (bonds). This provides predictable returns and has a minimal risk if the bonds are held to maturity. There is also a significant portion of assets held in cash (virtually risk free). A small amount of stocks are allowed to help increase the annual return of this portfolio.

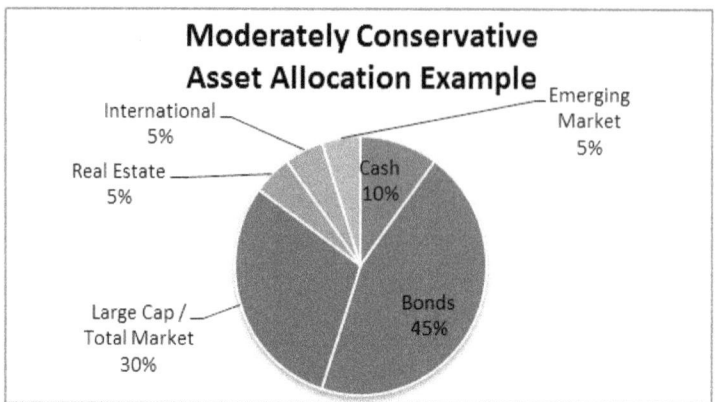

Figure 5.6.3 – A Moderately Conservative Asset Allocation Example

For the moderately conservative asset allocation, the bond and cash holdings are reduced and the funds moved mainly into large capitalization and/or total market index funds. We have also introduced a small allocation to emerging market index funds. This type of asset allocation will have a higher expected return than the conservative asset allocation over the long run.

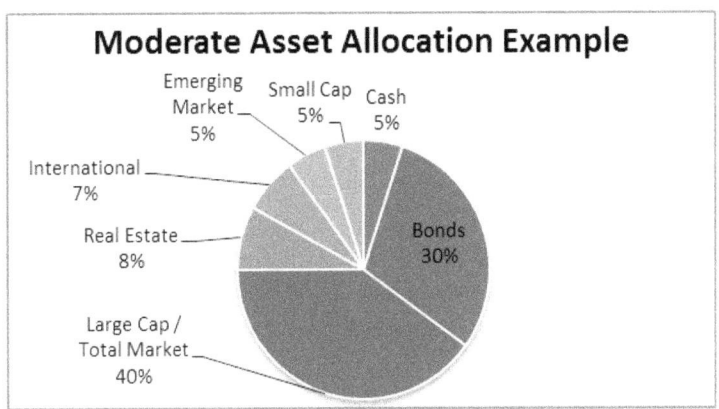

Figure 5.6.4 – A Moderate Asset Allocation Example

With a moderate asset allocation, bonds and cash are reduced to a greater extent. More funds are moved into the large capitalization and/or total market basket. Small capitalization stocks are added as a basket at this point.

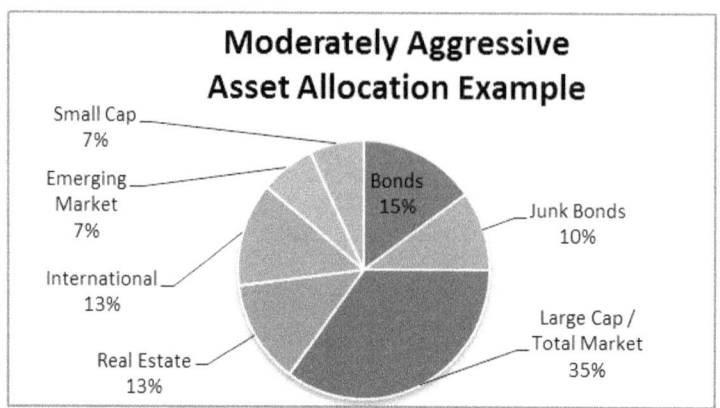

Figure 5.6.5 – A Moderately Aggressive Asset Allocation Example

    This moderately aggressive asset allocation example eliminates the cash holding portion all together. Some of the bond investment funds are moved from investment grade to "junk bonds." Junk bonds are riskier, but have a higher long term return. Investments in real estate, international stocks, emerging market stocks, and small cap are also increased.

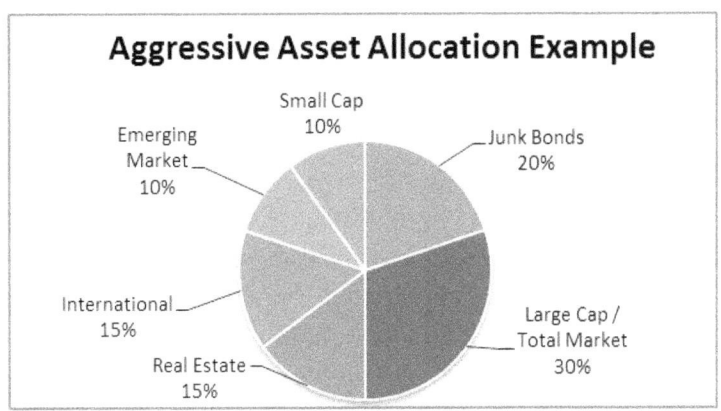

Figure 5.6.6 – An Aggressive Asset Allocation Example

Finally, the aggressive asset allocation example removes investment grade bonds all together in favor of junk bonds. Additional funds are taken from the large capitalization and/or total market and funneled into riskier investments.

To illustrate the investment performance difference between conservative, moderate, and aggressive asset allocations, refer to figure 5.6.7 below. The timeframe used in this figure is from 10/10/2007 (the previous market top) through present day (6/10/1014). I want to draw your attention to the market bottom that occurred in the 2008/2009 timeframe. The conservative asset allocation portfolio (presented in Figure 5.6.2) merely saw a 10% decrease in its value while the aggressive asset allocation portfolio (presented in Figure 5.6.6) saw a whopping 54% drop in its value! The aggressive asset allocation is not for the faint of heart!

Fast forward five years later and it becomes apparent that the extra risk of the aggressive asset allocation is paying off. The conservative asset allocation portfolio is up 28% while the aggressive asset allocation portfolio is up 44%! Note that the performance of the moderate asset allocation portfolio is merely a blend between the conservative and aggressive allocations.

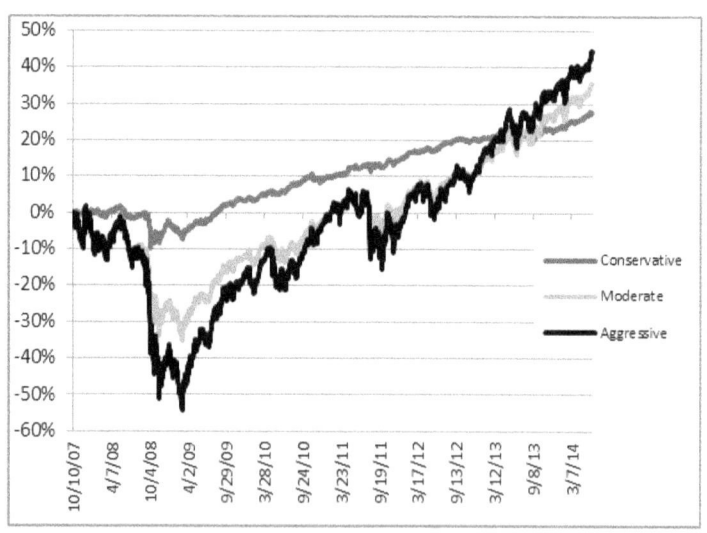

Figure 5.6.7 – Asset Allocation Performance Examples

Derek – I am lost. Please help me!

Repeat after me: everything is going to be OK. If all of this asset allocation stuff is still mumbo-jumbo to you, do not sweat it. Luckily, there is still a way for you to invest in the stock market without having to understand all of these complicated charts and figures. Investment companies have created a new investment vehicle called the "**target retirement fund**."

These target retirement funds are actually mutual funds that start out as aggressively allocated, shift their asset allocations to moderate, then to conservative as the target retirement date approaches. Just simply select the year range when you plan to retire, and everything else is taken care of for you. In Figure 5.6.8 below, I have created a table of popular target retirement funds for your consideration.

Note: I am presenting the Vanguard funds here because they charge the smallest fee ratio by far. Other firms charge anywhere from 0.77% - 0.85%! What a rip off!

Target Retirement Fund	Ticker	Expense Ratio
Vanguard Target Retirement 2020 Fund Investor Shares	VTWNX	0.16%
Vanguard Target Retirement 2025 Fund Investor Shares	VTTVX	0.17%
Vanguard Target Retirement 2030 Fund Investor Shares	VTHRX	0.17%
Vanguard Target Retirement 2035 Fund Investor Shares	VTTHX	0.18%
Vanguard Target Retirement 2040 Fund Investor Shares	VFORX	0.18%
Vanguard Target Retirement 2045 Fund Investor Shares	VTIVX	0.18%
Vanguard Target Retirement 2050 Fund Investor Shares	VFIFX	0.18%
Vanguard Target Retirement 2055 Fund Investor Shares	VFFVX	0.18%

Figure 5.6.8 – Target Retirement Fund Examples

This chapter discussed stock pricing and picking. I tried my best to persuade you that diversification through market index funds is the way to go. The chapter also conducted a crash course in asset allocation and looked at some real world asset location examples. This information should give you some ideas for constructing your own portfolio.

One of the final pieces of the stock market puzzle that requires consideration is **when** you should invest your hard-earned money. If you have a pile of cash, should you invest it all at once, or should you invest it a little bit at a time each month? Should you try to maximize your gains by buying low and selling high (timing the market by picking market tops and bottoms)? What about day trading and other more exotic derivative trading? Chapter 6 will jump feet first into answering all of these market timing related questions.

Chapter 6
WHEN SHOULD I BE INVESTING?

In the previous chapter, you saw what types of ETFs in which to invest. I hope that you have taken the time to plan out an asset allocation that will fit with your stock market investing needs. This chapter will cover topics of:

- **investing vs trading**
- **timing the market**
- **fundamental analysis**
- **technical analysis**
- **rebalancing.**

Once you finish this chapter, you will know more than 90% of the stock market investors out there, and I will bet you will have the long-term investment results to prove it. Let's get started!

6.1 – Investing vs. Trading

- **Investing** - Most definitions will tell you that investing is the purchase of an asset (or item) with the hope that it will increase in value over time or generate some type of income. Investing will typically involve purchasing an asset, holding it for some long period of time, and then selling the asset for a profit. Investing is usually used to refer to long-term planning and outlooks.
- **Trading** – Most definitions for trading appear to read strikingly similar to investing definitions. There is the anticipation of asset appreciation or some type of income, but trading carries one main difference with investing. Trading (or speculating) will typically have a very short time horizon.

Investing usually involves holding assets for years to decades. With trading, assets are usually held for anywhere from a few months to fractions of a second! Because trading is so focused on the time component, trading also involves high risk.

Which type of activity is right for you?

As you will find out in this chapter, if you are looking to become a trader then you have picked the wrong book! I hope to persuade you that trading is largely a waste of your time, and it can result in losing a lot of money even if you are careful. Please do NOT ask me how I arrived at this revelation!

Why do so many folks that initially start with stock market investing get drawn into the allure of trading, stock picking, and market timing?

I think it is because our culture "sells" day trading as a sexy, low-skill method to get rich quick. Think about it from a broker's or stock market news outlet's point of view. These companies profit when you actively trade, read articles, buy hot tips, and subscribe to newsletters!

Do these types of companies want you to buy a couple of assets and just let them sit there and appreciate over the years? Of course not! They make their money by encouraging you to move your money around. Hence, media outlets and advertisers slam you with constant stock upgrades, stock downgrades, stock market update reports, and hot stocks picks *ad nauseam*. These companies have a vested interest in turning you into a trader!

Derek, why do you believe that long-term investing is better than trading?

I have actually tried my hand at trading, and I failed miserably at it. This does not mean that you cannot be successful with trading, but let me cover some of the main reasons why I believe investing is to be preferred over trading:

- **80% of actively managed funds fail to beat S&P-500** – Numerous studies and reports over the years have shown that more than 80% of actively managed investment funds fail to beat the S&P-500 over a ten year period. When you extend the time-frame to thirty years trading is a disaster in most cases. This is even **before** taxes and fees are taken into account. After fees and taxes are taken into account, only about 2% of the managers are able to outperform the S&P-500 over thirty years. These are professionals that are paid millions of dollars a year to fight for the top performance. If 98% of these folks cannot beat the market over the long-term, what makes you think you can?
- **Taxes** – The long term capital gains tax rate you will pay is likely 15%. This is the tax you will pay on qualifying dividends and any stock that you sell at a profit that you have owned for more than one year. Guess what happens with trading? You will pay taxes on your profits as if it were ordinary income. For most of us, this will be somewhere in the range of 25% - 35%! No thank you!
- **Commissions** – Another nasty impact of trading is the higher commission bill that you will have to pay. With trades costing $2-$10 each way, this can add up very quickly if you are an active trader. These fees will serve to lower your overall return right off the bat regardless of your speculating performance.
- **Risk** – Trading will typically involve a much higher risk than investing. If you are investing for the next 10-30 years, bad news will look like a little blip on your 30 year chart of the overall market. Because traders are looking to make money quickly, they will often employ extreme amounts of **leverage**. This is great if you are on the "right side of the

trade" and make money, but if you guess wrong you can find your entire trading account wiped out in the blink of an eye. You could even end up owing the brokerage firm money! Have you ever experienced the feeling of losing $1,000 (or more) in less than one second?!? I have, and let me tell you – it was not fun at all. I enjoy making money rather than losing it.

- **Time** – With a strategy of investing in market index funds, your investments can be handled in about five minutes a month. With trading, the sky is the limit in terms of time required to try and outperform the millions of other "stock pickers" and "market timers" out there. It is not unusual to see folks spending 10-12 hours a week (or more) devoted to trading activities. Is this really how you want to be spending your free time?

- **High Frequency Trading (HFT)** – This list of negatives for trading would be getting long enough without the addition of HFT. What exactly is HFT? HFT is computer trading between themselves with millisecond delays. The advent of HFT means that not only do you have to beat out humans when you are trading, but currently a new wrinkle has developed. Now you are also competing against computers. These programs can parse through headlines and news in milliseconds and execute trades to take advantage of slight market movements. It is impossible for you to react faster than these machines; hence, as a trader you will always be one step behind the computers and riding the tail end of any market moves.

- **Stress** – For most individuals, all of these factors associated with trading tend to result in a high amount of stress placed on the individual trader. If you are in an important meeting and your particular trade is currently taking a massive beating, do you think you will be able to really concentrate and put in a good job performance? Not very likely.

- **Total devotion** – People that are willing to give total devotion to trading can, through enough practice, make a living at it and even develop respectable wealth. Unless you are willing to make trading a full time job, you really should be wary about jumping in the water. If you are not careful, you will end up as "fresh meat" for the computers and professionals. Many different studies and articles have all come to the same general conclusion. 95% of all new "day traders" will blow up their account (lose all their money).

OK, my intent here was to put a big scare into you when it comes to trading. Stock market trading really is only for a very select few. Most that get involved in it will lose all of their money or underperform the general stock market over the long run. Unless you have aspirations to become a professional Wall Street trader, I would stay very far away from this activity.

With your new and improved grasp of stock market trading, let's move onto a more general discussion of timing the stock market.

6.2 – Timing the Market – Bull and Bear Markets

In this section of the book, I hope to persuade you that attempts to time the stock market are a fool's errand that is best left to TV personalities and others that buy into this type of mumbo-jumbo. I only wish I had learned early on that it is nearly impossible to time the market consistently over a lifetime of stock market investing.

What exactly is timing the market?

Timing the stock market is when you try to buy stocks at a low point and then turn around and sell them at a high point. This would be great if it were always possible to be this lucky– think about it. You would stand to make four or five times as much (or more) over a lifetime if you could buy into the stock market at the very end of a major downturn and sell out right at the moment it hits the highs. In order to time the market effectively and consistently, you would have to outsmart the millions of other folks who are also playing the stock market trading "game."

Many financial books have likened timing the market to flipping a coin. Heads would represent a successful market timing attempt and tails would represent a losing marking timing attempt. Is it possible to flip a coin and have it land heads twice in a row? Of course! The chance of that happening is 25% (½ x ½ = 25%). How about flipping heads five times in a row? The chances of that are a little over 3%.

If we assume that the average **bull market** (more on that in a bit) lasts five years and the average bear market last three years, this gives us an eight year market cycle. Let's assume that you will be investing money from the age of 20 until you are 85. This gives us 65 years of investing at our fingertips. Now, if the average bull/bear cycle is eight years, then each of us will have about eight major chances in our lifetimes to try to time the macro-market.

However, in order to time the stock market successfully, you need to predict the top AND the bottom accurately. This doubles the amount of times we will need to be correct to 16 (65 years / 8 cycles X 2 opportunities per cycle = ~16). What are the chances of flipping a coin and having it land heads sixteen times in a row? The chance of this happening is only about 0.0015% or a one in 65,536 chance!

The coin flipping example I gave is greatly oversimplifying how the whole process of timing the stock market would work in real life, but I think it gives you a pretty good picture for just how difficult it is to remain successful at this practice. The odds are very similar if you attempt to correctly time the market over a lifetime. The bull markets (times when the market is increasing overall) never last exactly five years. Bear markets (times when the market is decreasing overall) never last exactly three years. Some bull markets extend and go seven or eight years themselves. Some bear markets are severe and quick and only last a year and a half or less. Unless you can time the stock market perfectly, you are much more likely to sell out prematurely or wait too long to start buying when the stock market participants finally capitulate and stock prices hit rock bottom.

Timing the stock market is a game played by millions of people around the world. As such, the odds are terribly stacked against you that you will find some way to outsmart nearly all of them. Simply put, the global stock markets cannot be predicted in the short run. Any attempt boils down to nothing more than an advanced form of gambling. It is better not to play the stock market timing game at all and just slowly and steadily invest your money over time.

Why does slow and steady investing "win the race?"

If you analyze historical stock market data for the US, you can see that if you pick any 30-year period of time, the stock market will always show an appreciation in value over this long term with dividends reinvested. This means that over the long run, the stock market is biased to increase in value. You can use this key information to your advantage to grow your wealth steadily over time. By ignoring the day-to-day fluctuations of the stock market, you can simply buy market index funds monthly (or quarterly). This approach will allow you to efficiently invest your money and grant peace of mind that your investments will see long term success. This simple method of investing, termed **dollar cost averaging**, is a proven method for stock market investing success.

How can we be so sure that dollar cost averaging will grant us investing success?

The concept of dollar cost averaging (or DCA) means that you will plan to invest a set amount of money in each period (usually monthly). Assume you plan to invest $1,000 from your monthly income each month in the stock market. Additionally, assume that at the beginning of the first month the market index fund you plan to purchase is selling for $100 a share. This means you will purchase 10 shares. Now, if at the end of the next month the stock market is a little higher than the previous month, your $1,000 will not go quite as far. If the price per share increases to $107, you could purchase only nine shares with your $1,000 (9.34 shares). On the other hand, if the market index fund drops in value down to $90 a share, now you will now be able to purchase 11 shares.

In this way, DCA means that you will buy more stock shares when the price drops and less shares when the price increases. This method of investing is a simple yet effective way to achieve long term successful stock market returns.

What if instead of investing monthly, you have a large lump sum of money that you would like to invest in the stock market? Let's say you just inherited $100,000. Should you invest all of this money right now, or should you invest a little bit at a time and dollar cost average into all of your stock market purchases?

This is a tricky question, as there are really no "right" answers. Instead of answering it directly, I will give you the pros and cons of investing it all now versus a little bit at a time. Let's begin with the scenario where you invest it all now.

It is impossible to time the market, further the market is generally biased to increase over the long run. Does this suggest it makes sense to invest all of it now? I would say it depends…

If you have previous stock market investing experience, or you have suffered through at least one bear market without freaking out, then you are ready to invest the lump sum immediately. If you have not been through at least one bear market, then you may not be ready to invest the entire lump sum. I would not want you to freak out when you saw a 30% - 50% drop in the market causing you to sell all your stock market shares for a huge investments loss. You would need just a little bit of experience under your belt to ensure that something like this will not happen to you emotionally.

This is the primary argument for dollar cost averaging if you have a large lump sum of money to invest. You may decrease your long term returns by slowly investing the money in the stock market, but there are many upsides to this method. Say you develop a plan to invest your $100,000 in the stock market over the course of two years. This will give you a chance to learn more about investing, gain experience, and potentially experience the emotions that are involved with a bear market. Remember, investing is a long term marathon, not a sprint. It will not do you one lick of good to invest all of the money on day one to squeeze out a little bit more return if you panic when the bear market hits and lock in permanent, substantial losses.

In the end, when you decide to invest your money in the stock market is completely your decision. For most folks that do not have a lump sum of savings or have not had a large inheritance drop in their lap, the only real option will be DCA. This is because they will be investing the savings generated from their income on a monthly basis. Others that do have a large sum of money to invest will have to make their own stock market investing decision based on their risk tolerance and investing experience.

The next two sections of this book will cover some more advanced methods for trying to time the market. I really hesitated to include this information as I am so opposed to timing the market, but I felt that the book would be incomplete if I ignored the subject altogether. You are sure to run across both of these topics out in the wild, so it is better I discuss them briefly so I can give you the inside scoop.

6.3 – Timing the Market – Fundamental Analysis

There are two main methods for attempting to identify major tops and bottoms of stock markets or individual stocks. The first of these methods is called fundamental analysis. This section of this book will be devoted to this method. First I will explain what fundamental analysis is and how it is used. Second, I will try to persuade you that fundamental analysis should really be approached cautiously. It can be helpful at picking good companies and times to invest in the market; then again, it can just as easily go wrong and lead you astray. As with all types of market timing and stock picking, I think this method is a real time-sink and does not produce positive results over the long run.

*What exactly is **fundamental analysis**?*

Fundamental analysis is a quantitative method (uses numbers) to attempt to identify assets that are underpriced. The theory of using this analysis is that if you can identify a fair market price for a stock or overall market, then when the price dips below this point it represents a "good investment deal."

Let's say we have a company called Larry's Buggy Whips and we are back in the 1800s. If you would like to determine a fair price to pay for one share of Larry's Buggy Whip stock, where should you start?!? Since you are interested in Larry's Buggy Whip stock specifically, you will need a bottom-up type of approach to calculate the fair price for one share of Larry's Buggy Whip stock.

The most popular fundamental analysis method used in a bottom-up approach is the dividend discount model (DDM). *What the heck is the DDM and how is it used?*

Let's explore how we can apply the DDM to Larry's Buggy Whips stock to calculate a fair market value. We saw in section 3.1 of this book and chapter 5 that investors purchase stock because they eventually expect to be compensated in the form of dividends. These anticipated earnings are really the only thing that gives a stock value (besides the assets of the company itself). So, if you wanted to take a whack at estimating the fair market value of a company's stock, you would have to come up with some sort of method to help estimate the future dividend payments by the company.

This whole process is pretty complicated and definitely outside the scope of a newbies book, but let me make some general comments. Analysts estimate the future dividends that a company will eventually deliver using the following assumptions:

- Dividend the company will eventually payout (if it has not already started paying out dividends). If the company is currently paying a dividend, then this value is known.
- Future stock market return above the risk free rate of return (this will be the overall predicted stock market return minus the 10-year treasury note yield)
- Future beta of the stock (how risky the stock in question is in relation to the overall market)
- Dividend growth rate for the company

As you can see, the entire process is based on a whole lot of assumptions!!! *How do analysts arrive at all of their assumptions?*

Analysts will typically examine a company's past financial statements to analyze revenue, expenses, assets, liabilities, and other financial characteristics of the company. They will also take global economic factors into account such as interest rates, inflation, GDP growth rates, exchange rates, energy prices, and productivity.

This financial data will be used as a basis to form the assumptions highlighted above. Analysts will then take these assumptions they have made and plug them into a formula which calculates what all those future dividend payments out into infinity will be worth in today's dollars. This is the **dividend discount model** (DDM) in a nutshell. It estimates the fair market price of the stock based on the current value of the future stream of dividends that will be generated.

Below in Figure 6.3.1, let's look at a couple examples to show how small variations in the assumptions that analysts make provide widely different fair market values for Larry's Buggy Whip stock.

	Case 1	Case 2	Case 3	Case 4	Case 5
Current Dividend =	$ 0.50	$ 0.50	$ 0.50	$ 0.50	$ 0.50
Future Beta of Stock =	1.0	1.0	0.9	1.0	1.2
Future Stock Market Return Above the Risk Free Rate of Return =	7.0%	7.5%	7.0%	7.0%	9.0%
Dividend Growth Rate =	4.5%	4.5%	4.5%	3.5%	2.5%
Fair Market Value of Stock =	$20.00	$16.67	$27.78	$14.29	**$ 6.02**

Figure 6.3.1 – Fair Market Values using DDM

In case #1 in Figure 6.3.1, assume that Larry's Buggy Whips is currently paying a $0.50 annual dividend, the future beta of the stock is 1.0, the future overall stock market return above the risk free rate of return will be 7%, and the dividend growth rate for Larry's Buggy Whips will be 4.5% annually. Using the DDM, this provides a fair market value for the stock of $20/share.

For case #2, it is assumed that the long term stock market return above the risk free rate of return is actually a little higher - 7.5% in this case. What happened to the fair market value price for Larry's Buggy Whip stock now? The DDM calculation shows us that the fair value for Larry's Buggy Whip stock is only $16.67/share!

With case #5 I decided to take the analysis to the extreme. It is assumed that stock's beta increases (the stock becomes riskier), and the stock market heats up. Larry's Buggy Whips has a lower dividend growth rate because with the advent of the motorcar buggy whips will become redundant. The fair market value is now about $6/share for the stock!! Crazy!

Millions of people base their investing decisions on this type of analysis, estimation, and prediction. When analysts issue a "buy" rating for a stock, they are indicating that the stock is currently priced below their calculated fair market value. Likewise, when an analyst issues s "sell" rating, the stock's current price is above their calculated fair market value.

I feel that the DDM is a bunch of hog wash and has no place forming my investment decisions. I will let you decide for yourself if you think this type of analysis is legit, or if you think it is for the dogs. To me, it equates to little more than reading tea leaves. As you can see from the example above, slight changes in assumption can produce a value of $20/share or only $6/share - a 333% difference.

What if we take the reverse approach and employ a top-down methodology?

In this case, analysts will start with the same information: interest rates, inflation, GDP growth rates, exchange rates, energy prices, and productivity. They will then go a step further and narrow the search down to a particular region or industry that they believe will show exceptional growth. Analysts will then try to determine which companies will show the best performance based on a detailed review of their current and past financial statements.

Compared to the bottom-up approach, the top-down approach does not work in the long run for all of the same reasons. There are too many assumptions and too many guesses as to what the future will hold! Do you think back in the 1800's anyone would have predicted that the buggy whip industry was about to become non-existent?!? It is hard to say, but I would seriously doubt it.

In the end, fundamental analysis boils down to nothing more than fancy guess work. This guesswork can be applied to individual stocks or broad global markets. Sometimes analysts will be able to guess correctly, and other times fundamental analysis will cause all who follow it to fail horribly with their investing. Because fundamental analysis is so hit-or-miss in terms of accurately helping investors to time the market, I suggest that you largely ignore it and tune out analysts' recommendations.

6.4 – Timing the Market – Technical Analysis

The second main method used to identify major tops and bottoms in specific stocks or the broader stock market is called **technical analysis**. *What exactly is technical analysis, and how is it used in stock market investing?*

Let me take you for a stroll down Technical Analysis Lane. Technical analysis is a form of timing the market based on stock market price movement patterns. The basic theory is that stock price patterns repeat themselves over and over again. If price movement in the past followed a certain pattern and resulted in a stock market price move, then the same thing is likely to occur in the future if similar patterns are experienced. It is nothing more than a method of stock price prediction based on historical price patterns.

Does technical analysis work to give an investor a market timing advantage? The short answer is: no, not really! The long answer is: it works some of the time, other times it falls completely flat on its face. This is no different than if someone developed a new and innovative way to tell if coin flips would land on heads or tails based on earlier previous flips.

You cannot predict random events with a set formula or pattern. No matter how hard you try, it is just not possible over the long term! Even if you could, once others caught onto the new system it would cease to work. Why is this the case? If everyone knew about the new "wonder predictor" they would be trying to jump ahead of everyone else to benefit personally. This would negate any predictive effects of the new "wonder predictor."

The tricky thing about technical analysis is that it is great "Monday morning quarter-backing". A set of parameters can almost always be found that will accurately predict winning trades when working with historical data. The problem is that when any type of model is tested going forward, it becomes less and less effective into the future. This is because the stock market price movements are largely random in nature. Technical analysis is like driving your car by focusing solely on the rear view mirror. The farther and farther you get down the road, the greater the chance things will not end pretty for you.

Humans are destined to believe they can predict random events based on patterns. We cannot help it; our minds are just wired to invent patterns to fit random data. Some folks who immerse themselves in technical analysis and become experts at it can find a way, through a combination of luck and skill, to achieve success. But, this takes a level of commitment that is akin to a full-time job. After all, you would be trying to stay ahead of the millions of competitors out there. For us ordinary stock market investing folks, we need something simpler that will work without requiring such a huge time commitment.

The next mini-section will take a look at some of the more popular technical patterns that traders use to attempt to get a leg up on the competition. Because this is a newbies book, I will just be scratching the surface of technical analysis. I hesitate to spend much time on this stuff because it really is like playing with fire. Most investors who trade trying to use technical analysis to make a quick buck will end up getting severely burned. If you really have no interest in technical analysis and trust that it is a waste of your time, then go ahead and jump forward to section 6.5 of this book. Otherwise, hold onto your hats...

6.4.1 **Range** – A simple pattern where the price of a stock bounces between two price levels. If a stock breaks out of a price range, the usual movement it about half to the full range of the channel size.

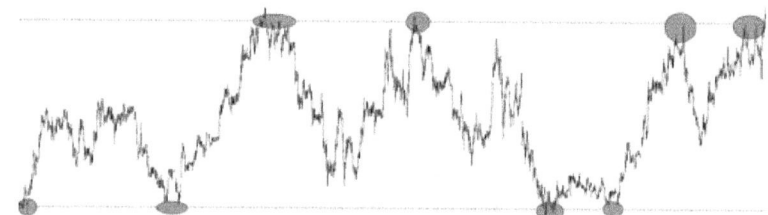

Figure 6.4.1 – Range Example

6.4.2 **Channel** – This is a simple pattern which is very similar to a range. The only difference is that the range will have an incline. A channel can be ascending (going up) or descending (going down). If a stock breaks out of a channel, it is hard to estimate exactly how far the price will move.

Figure 6.4.2a – Ascending Channel Example

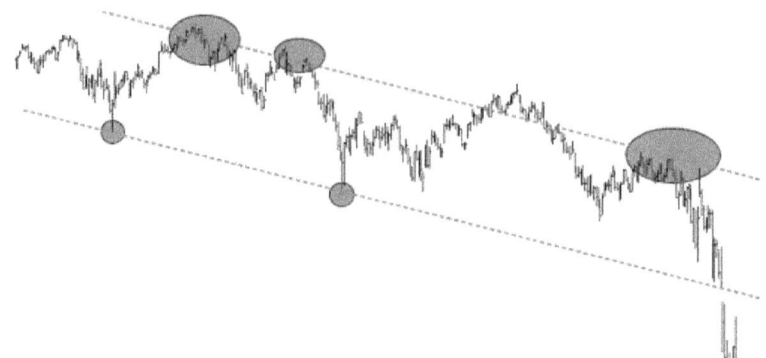

Figure 6.4.2b – Descending Channel Example

6.4.3 **Cup & Handle** – This is where the price movement hits up against a price resistance (like a ceiling) and then drops back down. If the price moves back up and breaks the resistance level, it will head higher. The usual movement is size of the "cup."

Figure 6.4.3 – Cup & Handle Example

6.4.4 **Head & Shoulders** – This interestingly
named pattern actually looks like a head and
shoulders. These can be topping patterns or
continuation patterns (price will continue to
increase if neckline is not pierced). If the
neckline is broken, price is expected to move
down by the amount of the distance from the
neckline to the head. Inverse head and
shoulders are a similar pattern – they are just
flipped upside down. In this case price is
expected to move higher if the neckline is
broken. These can also be bottoming
patterns, or continuation patterns (price will
continue to decrease if neckline is not
pierced).

Figure 6.4.4a – Head and Shoulders Example

Figure 6.4.4b – Inverse Head and Shoulders Example

6.4.5 **Bull Flag and Bear Flag** – A bull flag is a consolidating pattern – the market takes a short "breather" before it continues its move higher. A bear flag is just the opposite – the market is taking a break from its decent before it begins the next drop. These flags are characterized by a "flag pole" followed by a small channel in the opposite direction of the flag pole.

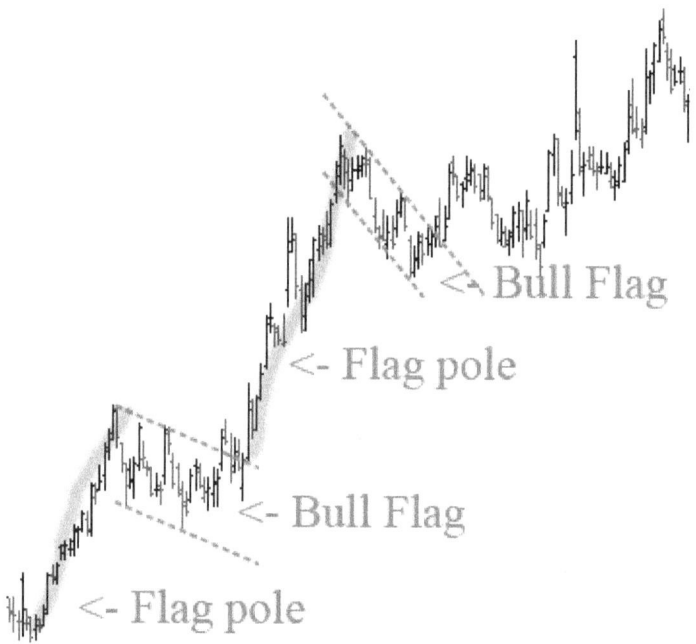

Figure 6.4.5a – Bull Flag Example

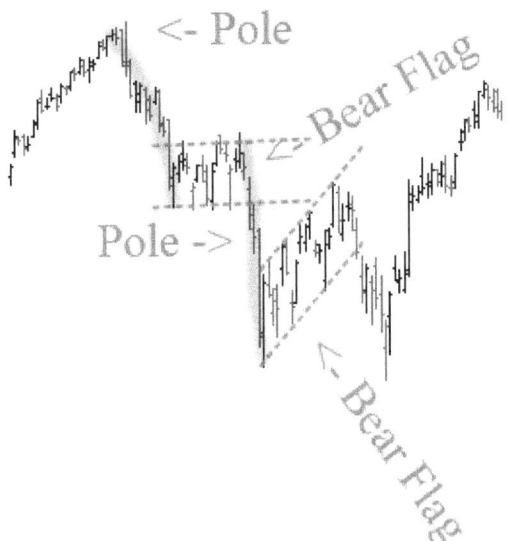

Figure 6.4.5b – Bear Flag Example

6.4.6 **Double Top and Double Bottom** – A double top is when an important price resistance level is hit and the stock or market corrects (moves down in price). A double top is a topping pattern. Similarly, a double bottom is when an important price support level is hit and the stock or market turns around and goes higher. A double bottom is a bottoming pattern.

Figure 6.4.6a – Double Top Example

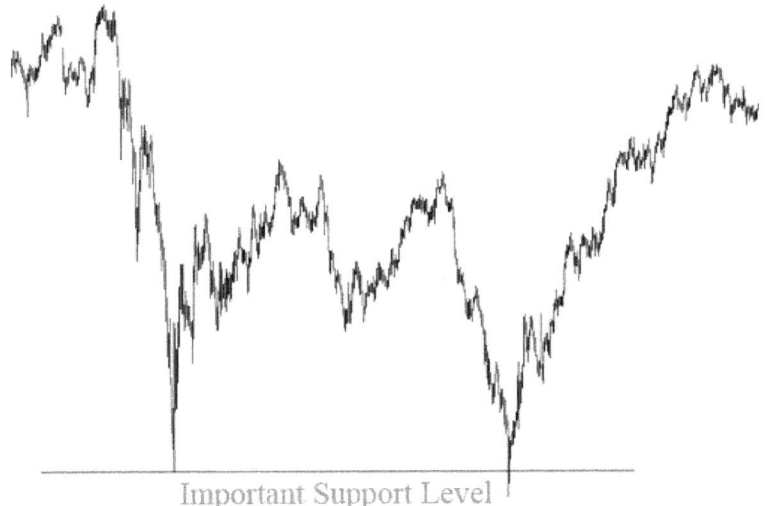

Important Support Level

Figure 6.4.6b – Double Bottom Example

6.4.7 **Moving Averages Cross** - A moving average is a technical analysis calculation used to "smooth out" price movements. The calculation will usually take the previous 20, 50, 100, or 200 closing prices and average these together. The value of this calculation is then plotted as a line on the price graph. A shorter term moving average, like the 20-day moving average, will move much more quickly if stock prices change than something like a 100-day moving average. If a short term moving average crosses above a longer term moving average, this indicates a "buy signal" because the stock is moving up quickly relative to its longer term price. Similarly, if the shorter period moving average crosses below a longer term moving average, then this generates a "sell signal" because the stock is moving down more quickly than its longer term price history. In the example below (Figure 6.4.7), the red line is the 20-day moving average and the blue line is the 50-day moving average.

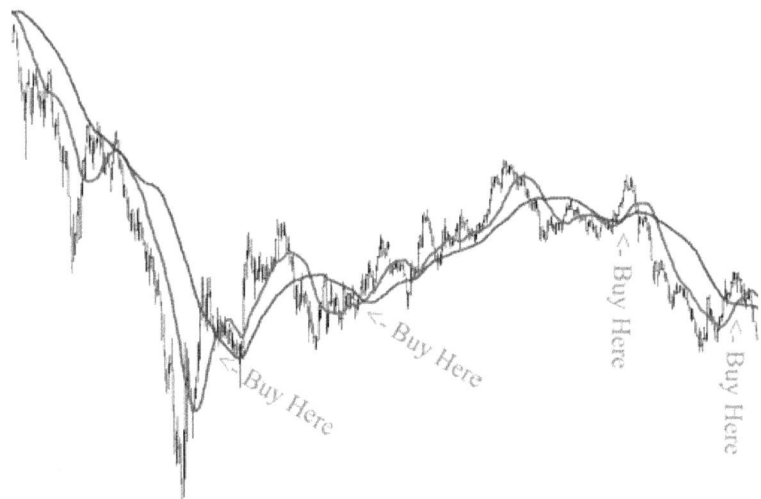

Figure 6.4.7 – Moving Averages Cross Example

6.4.8 **Moving Averages Support/Resistance** – Common moving averages such as the 100-day or the 200-day moving average can also serve as support or resistance for a stock or the overall market. This is because many investors keep an eye on this technical indicator for longer term investing. Below in Figure 6.4.8, the 200-day moving average is shown. Notice how it can serve as resistance (preventing price from rising above it) and support (preventing price from falling below it).

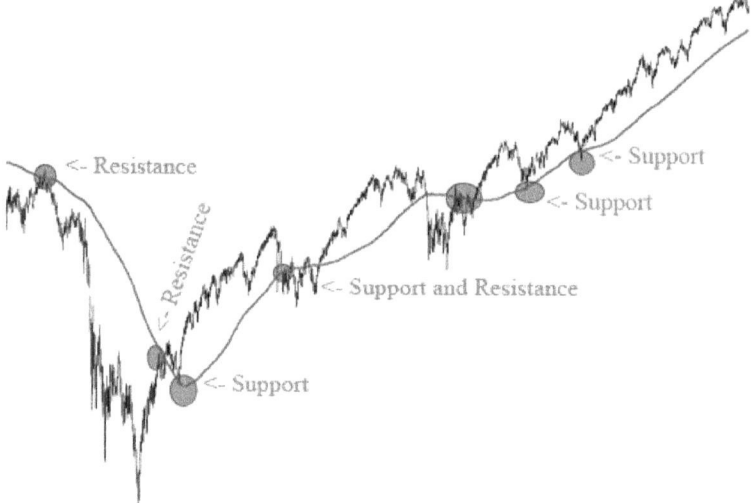

Figure 6.4.8 – Moving Averages Support/Resistance Example

6.4.9 **Relative Strength Index (RSI)** – The RSI is a technical indicator that is a type of momentum oscillator. There are literally dozens of these types of technical indicators built into stock charting platforms, but this is one of the most popular. I will touch on the RSI and one other type of oscillator because this is a newbies book. I do not want to bore you to death or confuse you with the details of dozens of different "tricks" that attempt to outsmart the other traders out there.

The RSI calculates stock price momentum as the ratio of higher closes to lower closes in a stock. Stocks that have stronger increases in price will show a higher RSI than stocks that are just floundering around in price. Likewise, stocks that are rapidly dropping in price will have a lower RSI. The RSI is usually plotted on a 14 day time-frame on a scale of 0 to 100. A RSI above 70 (the upper horizontal line) usually indicates that a stock is "overbought" and may soon fall to lower prices. A RSI value below 30 (lower horizontal line) usually indicates that a stock is "oversold" and may bounce higher.

Red Arrows = Sell Signal

Green Arrows = Buy Signal

Figure 6.4.9 – RSI Example

6.4.10 **Bollinger Bands** – Bollinger Bands are the other type of technical indicator of the momentum oscillator variety that I will cover. These bands are used to measure the "lowness" or "highness" of the current stock price relative to previous prices. They are basically volatility indicators that use moving averages and standard deviations. The presumption is that if the stock price moves to touch a band or moves outside of the bands, it will "snap" back in the opposite direction and revert back to the average.

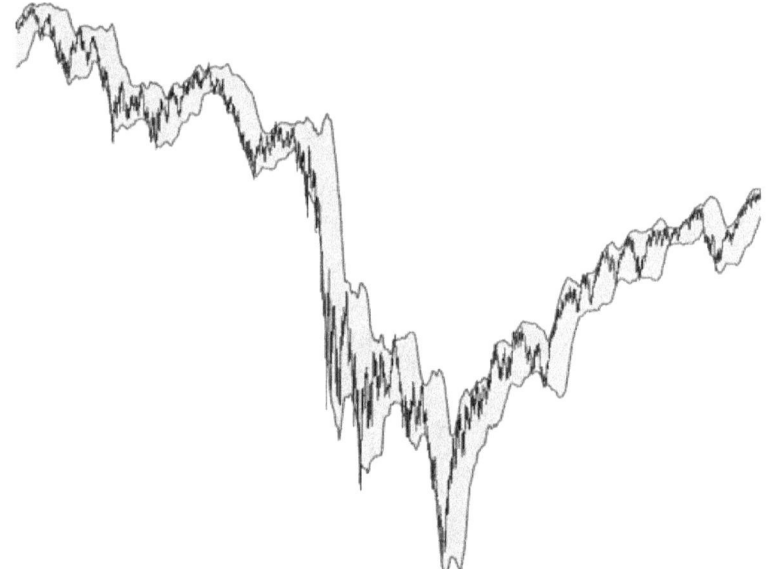

Figure 6.4.10 – Bollinger Bands Example

I have covered ten different types of technical analysis patters/indicators. There are literally hundreds of price patterns and elaborate technical indicators out there available for you to use in real time. Many of these will work some of the time. Other times, they will not work at all and cause you to lose substantial amounts of money if you put your full faith into them. The theory is that proper application can set you up for a high potential gain with a small, defined risk. Technical analysis is really best left to the five percent of folks that can devote their lives to trading each and every day. The other 95% of us want to avoid trading like the plague because it really is just a recipe for financial loss.

I hope that is the last time you ever have to hear about RSIs or Inverted Head and Shoulders! Are there any market timing concepts that are actually semi-legitimate and will not take our entire day to implement? Yes! There is a market timing concept that I would like to cover that actually is worth our while to discuss and include in your stock market investing toolbox. It is now time for us to cover the basics of portfolio rebalancing.

6.5 – Timing the Market – Rebalancing

What is rebalancing and what does it have to do with stock market investing?

Rebalancing is an easy way to get your portfolio back in line with your target asset allocation that we set in Chapter 5 of this book. Just what the heck does that mean exactly, and how can it help you with your investing? Let's look at a simple example.

As an example, I will assume you have set a very simple asset allocation at the beginning of the year. For your asset allocation, you have decided to put half of your $20,000 of investment money into bonds and the other half into stocks. Figure 6.5.1 below illustrates your asset allocation at the beginning of the year.

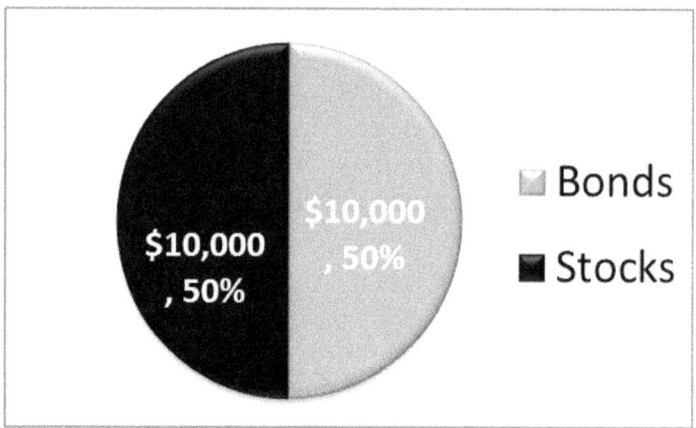

Figure 6.5.1 – Starting Asset Allocation

Next, I will assume that you made it to the end of the year and the stock portion of your portfolio has performed spectacularly. Your stocks were up a whopping 45% for the year. I will assume that the bond portion of your portfolio was up only 3%. This now means that the stock portion of your portfolio actually makes up 58%

($14,500) of your portfolio versus the target asset allocation of just 50% - see Figure 6.5.2.

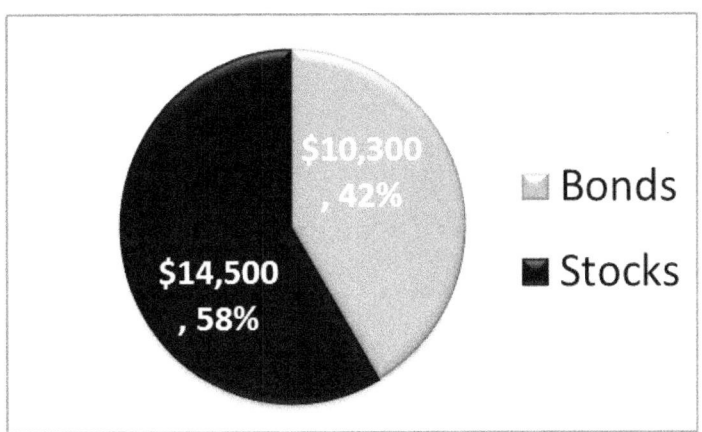

Figure 6.5.2 – New Asset Allocation after Good Year

If you do nothing to adjust your portfolio back to the original asset allocation, it will be weighted much more significantly towards stocks. Because of this, your portfolio will actually be taking on more risk going forward. This is because your portfolio now has a higher allocation towards riskier types of investments (stocks) versus the more conservative types of investments (bonds).

What are the options for your portfolio now that we are at the end of the year?

You could either accept that your portfolio is more risky and leave everything alone, or you could adjust your portfolio to return things back to your original planned asset allocation of 50% bonds and 50% stocks.

We call this adjustment back to your target asset allocation **rebalancing**. The best way for you to rebalance things back to the 50/50 asset allocation would be to sell $2,100 of stocks and use that money to buy $2,100 more of bonds. Your portfolio now would look like this:

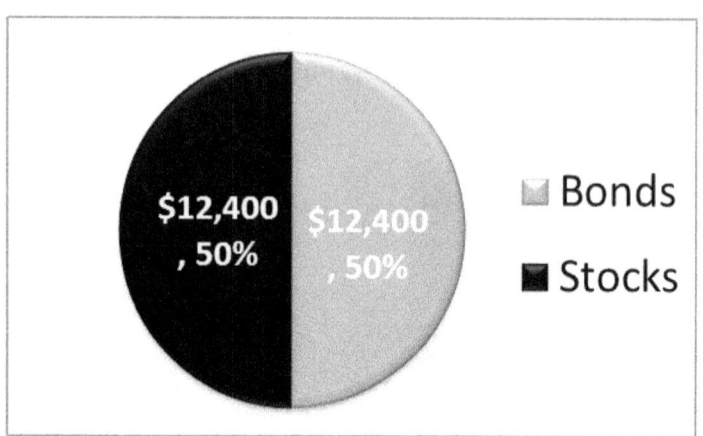

Figure 6.5.3 – Rebalanced Portfolio at End of Good Year

Why would an investor want to go to all this trouble of buying and selling assets to rebalance their portfolio?

There are two main reasons:

1.   **Maintain the target portfolio risk** – By rebalancing your portfolio on a set schedule, you can reset the amount of risk your portfolio is taking back to what it originally was when you selected your particular starting asset. As alluded to earlier, if the stock portion of your portfolio increases greatly and nothing is done to rebalance things, your overall portfolio will be inherently riskier going forward. This is generally viewed as unfavorable by investors because everyone wants to maintain a comfortable amount of portfolio risk. The exact opposite can also be the case – if the stock portion of your portfolio drops so that it is lower than your target allocation, your portfolio might not be taking on enough risk. If nothing is done to correct this, then the portfolio could potentially earn

lower returns going forward (lower risk gives lower return).

2. **Increase returns** – By rebalancing your portfolio on a set schedule, you are also going through the exercise of "buying low" and "selling high." Assets that have increased in value relative to other assets in your portfolio will become "over-weighted." In order to set things right, it is necessary to sell the "over-weighted" assets and purchase the "underweighted" assets. This will serve to increase your returns over the long run when investing in the stock market. Many sources that have analyzed rebalancing claim a generalized 1% - 2% increase in average annual returns when rebalancing is performed on a set schedule.

What is a good frequency to rebalance one's investment portfolio?

You may have noticed by now, but so far I have been suggesting that one rebalances their portfolio "on a set frequency." I have left this intentionally vague until now. A very intelligent question! There are several reasons why you should NOT rebalance your portfolio more often than once a year:

1. Short term capital gains taxes kick in on profit from investments held shorter than one year. Capital gains taxes are discussed in more detail in Chapter 7.
2. Transaction fees to buy and sell assets add up quickly. If you are working with an asset allocation that maintains 8-10 (or more) stocks, these charges can really drain your overall portfolio performance when you are just getting started.

3.　　Rebalancing does take a bit of a time commitment. Usually, about one hour is required to make the necessary adjustments. But, if you are trying to rebalance your portfolio monthly (the horror!) that time will take away from other things you could be doing.

4.　　The general markets and various assets tend to move in multi-year cycles in relation to each other. By rebalancing your portfolio more often than this, you are not really benefiting from this phenomenon.

In general, I agree with many investing experts that suggest the best frequency to rebalance a portfolio is in the range of **two** to **three** years. In doing so, this will allow you to:

- keep well outside of the short term capital gains window
- minimize your trading transaction costs
- minimize the necessary time requirements
- make adjustments at a frequency that will allow you to take advantage of the major shifts in the different markets.

What should we do if we are dollar cost average investing on a monthly frequency?

We can still use the same principle s for rebalancing to ensure we are "buying low." I will assume you have $1,000 each month to invest after all of your expenses, and you have identified a target asset allocation. Each month, you will analyze your current asset allocation and compare this to your target asset allocation. Whichever asset is the most under its target is the type of asset that you should purchase for that month. In this example below (see Figure

6.5.4), you would plan to purchase international stocks because it is the most "underweighted" at -0.9%.

	Target	Current	Difference
Bonds	60%	60.7%	0.7%
Large Cap	12%	11.3%	-0.7%
Real Estate	4%	4.9%	0.9%
International	4%	3.1%	**-0.9%**
Cash	20%	19.9%	-0.1%

Figure 6.5.4 – Using Rebalancing Concept When Dollar Cost Average Investing

If you follow this method of investment each month, you can ensure that you very closely follow our asset allocation. This will help to maintain the amount of risk that you planned for when you originally selected your target asset allocation. Additionally, if any one asset in your portfolio drops in value relative to the others due to a major market shift, this method will allow you to identify this and "buy low" when the opportunity presents itself.

In this chapter I discussed different methods of timing the market. I argued that **trading** in the stock market is really best left to the 5% who can devote their entire lives to this "profession." Hopefully, I persuaded you that attempting to time the market is a fool's errand. Finally, I made a case for a periodic rebalancing of your portfolio to maintain your selected risk/reward based on your chosen asset allocation. I have given you just about all the information you will need to go out on your own and survive as a stock market investor.

There are just a couple more miscellaneous topics I would like to cover with you in the final chapter. In Chapter 7 we will cover:

- how to best avoid the "tax man" when it comes to investing

- further suggested reading if you are interested in learning even more about investing

Chapter 7
FINAL THOUGHTS

We have just about run the gamut of the basic information a newbie will need to understand to intelligently invest in the stock market. This final chapter houses a couple of miscellaneous topics that I felt important to cover with you before I send you on your merry investing way. Here I will discuss:

- **taxes and investing**
- **suggest further reading if you are interested in gaining even more stock investing knowledge**
- **then I will release you into the wild!**

7.1 – Stock Market Investing and Taxes

Mark Twain remarked: "The only difference between a tax man and a taxidermist is that the taxidermist leaves the skin." If you are not careful when investing, the taxes from selling or owning certain types stocks can eat you alive! This section will give you the basic investing tax knowledge you will need to keep more green in your pocket.

The first type of tax that you need to be concerned with is **capital gains tax**. Capital gains tax is the tax you will pay on any investment profits when that investment vehicle (stocks, bonds, ETFs, Mutual funds, etc.) is sold. For example, say you bought 100 shares of Intel (INTC) stock at $18.00 a share and sold the stock later for $25.00 a share. You would owe capital gains tax on the $7.00 per share profit.

There are two types of capital gains taxes – short-term capital gains and long-term capital gains:

Short-term capital gains are taxed at the investor's ordinary income rate. These types of gains are applied to investments that are held *one year or less* before they are sold.

Long-term capital gains are taxed at a much lower rate and are applied to investments that are held *longer than one year* before they are sold. See Figure 7.1.1 below which illustrates the different tax rates for ordinary income, short-term capital gains, and long-term capital gains (Note: these figures are based on 2014 US tax rates).

Single Income Brackets	Joint Income Brackets	Ordinary Income Rate	Short-Term Capital Gains Rate	Long-term Capital Gains Rate
$0 - $8,925	$0 - 17,850	10%	10%	0%
$8,926 - $36,250	$17,851 - $72,500	15%	15%	0%
$36,251 - $87,850	$72,510 - $146,400	25%	25%	15%
$87,951 - $183,250	$146,401 - $223,050	28%	28%	15%
$183,251 - $398,350	$223,051 - $398,350	33%	33%	15%
$398,351 - $400,000	$398,351 - $450,000	35%	35%	15%
$400,001 +	$450,001 +	39.6%	39.6%	20%

Figure 7.1.1 – Short-Term and Long-Term Capital Gains Tax Rates

Note that long-term capital gains tax rates can be 10% - 20% lower than short-term capital gains rates! I have had friends who have literally sold their investments on the 362nd day of ownership because they did not understand the difference between short-term and long-term capital gains tax rates. Please do not be that person! You could end up paying thousands of dollars more in taxes over a lifetime if you do not understand this simple concept. Please check how long you have owned an investment before you sell it.

In our example above, the investor bought 100 shares of Intel (INTC) stock for $18.00 per share and later sold it for a profit at $25.00 per share. This sale would trigger a capital gain of $700.00. Let's assume she is in the

144

25% tax bracket and we owned the stock for 364 days. She would then owe $175 in short-term capital gains taxes for this transaction. Instead, had she sold this stock after owning it for 366 days, she would only owe $105 in taxes. $70 in extra taxes may not sound like a lot, but in this case it reduced her overall investment return from a 33% return to 29.2% return. A 3.8% drop in her portfolio's return is a really big deal as the size of her portfolio begins to grow!

You also need to pay attention to taxes when it comes to dividends. There are two types of stock dividend tax rates: **ordinary** and **qualified**. "Ordinary" stock dividend payments are taxed at your ordinary income rate (25%+ for most of us). "Qualified" stock dividend payments are taxed at the lower long-term capital gains rate providing certain qualifications are met:

- The dividend was paid after 12/31/2002 – there should be no problem here unless you have been experimenting with time travel.
- Paid by a **US corporation** or readily traded on an established US stock market.
- The stock was held for more than 60 days during the 121-day period that begins 60 days before the dividend ownership "cut-off" period is announced.

This can all be a little confusing if you own a lot of different stocks from around the world and are active trading in and out of positions. As a long-term investor, you only need to be concerned with the second bullet point highlighted above. Section 5.6 of this book suggested several potential ETFs that could be used to create a well-diversified portfolio. Figure 7.1.2 below highlights the percentage of the dividend each ETF pays out that will count as a "qualified" dividend.

Name	Ticker	% Qualified
Vanguard FTSE Developed Markets ETF	VEA	100%
Vanguard Total Stock Market ETF	VTI	100%
Vanguard Small-Cap Growth ETF	VBK	74%
Vanguard FTSE Emerging Markets ETF	VWO	57%
Vanguard Total Bond Market ETF	BND	0%
Vanguard REIT ETF	VNQ	0%

Figure 7.1.2 – Qualified Dividend Percentages

Smart investors can use the above information to their advantage to achieve even higher long-term returns. Certain types of ETFs, such as the bond market ETF and the REIT ETF, do not pay a qualified dividend at all (notice BND and VNQ above). This means that dividends from these types of investments are taxed as ordinary income (at the 25+% rate for most of us).

To squeeze the most out of your investment dollars, and pay the least amount of tax possible, it is advantageous to keep these types of investments in tax-deferred accounts such as a 401(k) or IRA. If you are able to hold bond ETFs and REIT ETFs in your retirement accounts, you will defer paying the higher "ordinary" taxes on the dividends, and you will also be able to reinvest the savings. This will help your 401(k) or IRA to grow even faster and will reduce the overall total amount of money you will end up paying in taxes! When you retire and are no longer earning a salary, you may be in a lower tax bracket and might not even need to pay any taxes on the required withdrawals from your IRA or 401(k)!

Although you do not plan to have losses in the stock market, I will cover the concept of a **capital loss** and its tax implications. A capital loss is incurred any time that you sell a stock for less than the purchase price. The IRS allows you to deduct up to $3,000 a year from your taxes if you incur a capital loss. A capital loss can also be carried forward multiple years until it has been fully deducted or offset by capital gains. As an example, assume that you sell stock and incur a $10,000 capital loss. If you incur no other capital gains, you will be able to deduct $3,000 a year for the first three years from your taxes. In the fourth year, you will be able to deduct the remaining $1,000 from your taxes.

7.2 – Further Reading

If you have read this book front-to-back, then you are more than equipped to begin stock market investing for the purposes of building your wealth. The information found in this book will be enough for 80% of the stock market investors out there. If you are interested in learning even more about personal finance, stock market investing, and the history of investing, I encourage you to read the following books:

- **I Will Teach You to Be Rich** – *$8-Workman Publishing Company* - This book written by Ramit Sethi is my favorite personal finance book of all time. Ramit starts by assuming you know nothing about personal finance and walks you through how to structure your finances to achieve wealth and become rich. It is a great beginner's book that I highly recommend.
- **The Four Pillars of Investing** – *$10-The McGraw-Hill Companies* - This intermediate level book written by William Bernstein covers the theory, history, psychology, and business of investing. Much of my inspiration came from this book. It is a great read if you are really looking to take your knowledge of investing to the next level. Just be sure you are ready to jump into a book that is 300+ pages.
- **A Random Walk Down Wall Street** – *$10-W.W. Norton and Company* - This is the most advanced book of the three recommended. Burton Malkiel gives a comprehensive review of stock market investing and really promotes the concept of market index fund investing. I also drew much inspiration from this book. Just be sure you have plenty of time on your hands before jumping in – this book is a whopping 449 pages!

7.3 – Bon Voyage!

Here we are – you have made it all the way to the end of this stock market investing for newbies book! My goal for this book was to create a stock market investing book that would be just right for the newbie. I wanted to create something that had good explanations and was accessible to the average investor. I hope that you found this book helpful and have committed to begin your journey into stock market investing today! Remember – every day that you put off investing is one more day that compound interest will not be able to work its magic for you.

If you enjoyed this book, please recommend it to a friend! If you have suggestions for improvement, please reach out to me and let me know what they are. Additionally, I would like to take this opportunity to welcome you to my personal finance blog: MoneyAhoy.com. Over at the blog I discuss topics such as: saving more money, making more money, and investment ideas. It really is a great collection of articles that discuss how you can work to build your wealth even faster. If you are interested in contacting me with questions, comments, or concerns, the best way to reach me is by email at: Derek.Chamberlain@MoneyAhoy.com.

You have now graduated from the ranks of newbie stock market investor. Congratulations and happy investing!

GLOSSARY

401(k) – A defined-contribution retirement plan where companies will typically match the employee's contribution dollars up to a fixed maximum percentage. Funds are invested tax-free, but taxes are due when the investments are withdrawn at retirement age.

Actively Managed Fund – A fund where the manager seeks to pick and choose specific investments that will perform better than the overall market.

Aggressive Growth – Investments that are typically more risky. Stocks that are aggressive growers will typically reinvest retained earnings to grow faster rather than paying out a dividend.

AMEX – The American Stock Exchange – the third highest volume of trading in the US takes place on this exchange. The majority of trading takes place with shares of small to medium-sized companies.

Annual Expense Ratio – The annual fee that mutual funds and ETFs charge their shareholders. This fee comes off the "top" before any profits in the mutual funds or ETF are realized.

Asset Allocation – The plan to divide investments into different asset categories such as stocks, bonds, real estate, and cash to optimize the risk/reward tradeoff based on an individual's risk tolerance.

Asset – A property or something of value that can be converted into cash.

Bear Market – A market in which the value of the object being traded is falling or expected to fall.

Bond – A loan with interest payments set to pay at some frequency (coupons). Typical bonds will have their principal paid back at the end of the loan (at maturity).

Broker – Comes in two versions: a full service broker or a discount broker. A full service broker is an actual person that will make investment suggestions and execute buy/sell orders at your request. A discount broker is an electronic system where you enter your own buy/sell orders through the computer.

Bull Market – A market in which the value of the object being traded is increasing or expected to rise.

Capital Gain – Profit resulting from the sale of real estate, stock, mutual funds, or other assets.

Capital Gains Tax – The type of tax applied to any type of capital gain incurred by an investor. This type of tax is not incurred until the asset is sold and the potential gain is realized.

Capital Loss – A loss resulting from the sale of real estate, stock, mutual funds, or other assets.

Commission – The fee that a broker will charge to conduct a buy/sell transaction for you.

Compound Interest – When the interest you earn on your principal also earns interest. In essence, it is interest earned on the previous interest earned.

Coupon – The interest rate stated on a bond when it is issued. Usually, the coupon is paid out to bondholders semiannually.

Day Trader – Buys and sells stock or other securities quickly. Attempts to generate profits based on small movements in the market. This activity will normally involve substantial leverage and risk.

Default Risk –The risk that the company, or government, may fail to make an interest payment on time.

Dividend Discount Model – A method of valuing the price of a stock using predicted future dividends and discounting them back to their present value.

Dividend – A distribution of a portion of a company's earnings to shareholders.

Diversification – The act of not "putting all of your eggs in one basket." The goal is to reduce risk and volatility in your portfolio by investing in different asset types which are unlikely to all move in the same direction at the same time.

Dollar Cost Averaging – A way to purchase more of an asset when it is cheaper and less of an asset when it is more expensive. One simply invests the same amount of money each period so that when price falls, one automatically purchases more.

Early Withdrawal Penalty – Applies to retirement accounts such as IRAs and 401(k)s. There is usually a 10% penalty, plus income taxes, when funds are pulled out before the age of 59 ½. There are some exceptions to the penalty such as first-time home purchases or education costs.

Earnings Per Share – How much profit a company has made per share of outstanding stock within a given period (usually updated each quarter). This is usually meaningless in and of itself because the company can control the number of outstanding stock shares, but it is useful in comparing quarter to quarter or year to year.

Emerging Market Fund – Funds that contain stocks from countries that have "young" stock and bond markets. Examples include the BRIC countries – Brazil, Russia, India, and China. These funds typically carry higher risk and higher reward.

ETFs – Exchange traded funds are a broad class of funds that trade throughout the day over an exchange. ETFs will generally have low expenses, but commissions apply to buy and sell them. They are typically more tax-efficient than mutual funds because of the way they process buying/selling of shares.

Expense Ratio – The annual fee that mutual funds and ETFs charge their shareholders. This fee comes "off the top" before any profits in the mutual fund or ETF are realized.

Fill-or-Kill Order – This is an "all or none" type of order. It instructs the broker to fill the entire order immediately or kill (cancel) the entire order. This type of order can be particularly useful when making large purchases in illiquid securities.

Fixed Income Securities – Securities that pay a set rate of return such as bonds. These types of investments provide a predictable stream of income.

Fundamental Analysis – Analysis of securities based on publically available information such as sales, expenses, revenue, dividends, and growth rates. This analysis is used to estimate the fair market value of a security.

Good-till-Canceled Order – An order to buy or sell a security that will remain in effect until it is either canceled or executed.

Growth Stock – Stock of companies that are showing higher than average growth in their earnings over the past several years. The belief is that these stocks have the potential for a higher than average future profit growth.

Individual Retirement Account (IRA) – A tax advantaged retirement investing account that comes in two varieties. A traditional IRA uses "pre-tax" money and is tax-deferred (pay tax when money is withdrawn at retirement age). A Roth IRA uses "after-tax" money and allows for tax-free growth (withdrawals at retirement age are tax free).

Inflation – The persistent increase in the general price level of a good or service in an economy over time.

Initial Public Offering (IPO) – The initial sale of stock of a private company to the public.

Interest Rate Risk – This is the risk for bond owners that interest rates will change. The amount of risk is a function of the bond's time to maturity and the bond yield.

International Fund – A fund that invests in companies located anywhere outside of the investor's country. These are also known as foreign funds.

Investment – Anything that will hold its value and is likely to increase in value over time. The typical investments are stocks, bonds, precious metals, and real estate.

Junk Bonds – Bonds with a credit rating of BB or lower. Because these bonds carry a higher credit risk, they pay a higher yield. These types of bonds are also referred to as high-yield bonds.

Large Cap – Stands for "large capitalization." A company's market capitalization is the total market value of all of its stock. Any company with a market capitalization of more than $10 billion is normally considered large cap.

Leverage – The term used when an investor borrows money to magnify investing results by allowing them to purchase more shares of an asset.

Life-cycle Fund – These are funds that are created for investors of a specific age or specific time horizon for investing. One example would be a 2040 Target Retirement Fund.

Limit Order – An order to buy or sell a security at a specific price (or a better price). This type of order will guarantee price, but not execution of the order.

Liquid Net Work – This is the sum total value of all possessions that can be converted to cash quickly.

This typically excludes things like retirement accounts, real estate, and land.

Market Capitalization – This is the total equity market value of a company. A company's market capitalization can be calculated by taking the number of outstanding stock shares multiplied by the current market stock price.

Market Index Fund – Funds (usually a mutual fund or exchange-traded fund) that track an index of a specific financial market and attempt to match its return.

Market Order – An order to buy or sell a security immediately at the best currently available market price. This type of order will guarantee execution, but not price.

Money Market – The market for short-term types of securities like short-term bonds, treasury bills, and guaranteed investment certificates with less than a three-year maturity. Many banks offer these types of accounts that function similar to a savings account.

Moving Average – This is a calculation to analyze stock prices by creating a series of averages based on previous price data. Typical periods used are 20 days, 50 days, 100 days, and 200 days. In the 200 day example, the previous 200 days closing stock price is averaged together to obtain one number. This is then plotted on the price graph. Each day, the oldest day is removed from the data set and the most current day is added to the data set for the average calculation. This is why it is termed a "moving" average.

Mutual Funds – These are funds that pool investors' money together to purchase securities for investment. These funds are managed by a group of professionals which charge a management fee for their management of the fund.

NASDAQ – This acronym stands for the National Association of Securities Dealers Automated Quotations Systems. The NASDAQ is a computer system that provides pricing quotes for smaller securities that are not yet large enough to trade on the New York Stock Exchange (NYSE).

Net Worth – This is the sum total value of all possessions (stocks, bonds, real estate, etc.) minus all outstanding debts.

NYSE – The New York Stock Exchange is the oldest and largest stock exchange in the US. In terms of market capitalization, the NYSE is also the largest stock exchange in the world. The NYSE is located on Wall Street in New York City, New York.

Partial Fill – An order to purchase a security that is not completely executed. A certain portion of the order has been completed and remaining portion exists in the system as an open order.

Passively Managed Fund – A fund whose securities are chosen automatically to match an index or part of a market. There is no portfolio manager that is actively "picking" investments. As a result, annual fees for these types of funds tend to be much less than actively managed funds.

Price to Earnings Ratio (P/E Ratio) – A stock's current price divided by the company's earnings per share. Also referred to as the P/E Ratio. This ratio can be used to indicate if a stock is underpriced or overpriced in comparison to similar companies in the same industry.

Principal – The original amount of money invested or the face value of a bond.

Portfolio – A group of securities and other financial assets such as stocks, bonds, cash, mutual funds, ETFs, etc.

Rebalancing – A process of resetting your asset allocation back to your selected original mix by buying and selling investments.

REITs – A Real Estate Investment Trust is a company that owns and operates income-producing commercial real estate. Examples of real estate owned/operated could include: apartment buildings, warehouses, hospitals, shopping centers, hotels, and offices. A REIT is required by US law to distribute at least 90% of their taxable income back to investors (as dividends).

Return – The amount of money an investment will make for you above and beyond your principal invested. This is usually expressed as a percentage. If a $10,000 return made you $700 in one year, this would be a 7% annual return on your investment ($700/$10,000).

Risk – The potential of an investment having a return that is different than what is expected. This could include investments that lose some of all of their value. Investments that have a higher variability of return are said to have a higher degree of risk.

Risk Tolerance – The amount of investment return variability that a person is willing to withstand. The higher the risk tolerance, the more variability a person is willing to stomach without panicking and selling investments at a suboptimal price.

Roth IRA – A tax advantaged retirement investing account. A Roth IRA allows for tax-free growth (withdrawals at retirement age are tax free).

RSI – The relative strength index is a technical indicator used to analyze securities to determine advantageous points to buy or sell securities based on price movement. The RSI is a momentum indicator and measures the velocity and magnitude of price movements.

S&P-500 Index – The Standard & Poor's 500 index is a market index based on the market capitalization of 500 large companies that have stock listed on the NASDAQ or the NYSE. Many consider it one of the best representations of the US stock market.

Securities and Exchange Commission (SEC) – A government commission created by congress in 1934 to regulate the securities markets and protect investors.

Security – A tradable asset of any kind. Examples include: stocks, bonds, mutual funds, and ETFs.

Small Cap – Stands for "small capitalization." A company's market capitalization is the total market value of all of its stock. Any company with a market capitalization of less than $800 million is normally considered small cap.

Speculator – An investor who assumes a calculated risk in the marketplace with the intention of making a profit. Speculators are usually focused on realizing short term profits and very often use leverage to magnify their potential profit.

Stock – A stock is an ownership interest in a company. Stockholders are entitled to any profits generated by a company after employees, suppliers, and lenders are paid. Companies normally sell stock to help invest in assets and fund their business growth.

Stock Market – A market in which stock shares of publically traded companies are traded and issued over an exchange.

Stop Limit Order – An order that combines the aspects of a stop order and a limit order. The order will be executed at a specific price (or better) once a given stop price is reached.

Stop Order – An order to buy or sell stock when its price crosses a particular point.

Target Retirement Fund - These are actually mutual funds that start out as aggressively allocated, shift their asset allocations to moderate, then to conservative as the target retirement date approaches.

Tax Rate – The ratio at which a business or person is taxed. Tax rates in the US range anywhere from 0% - 39.6% depending on the amount and type of income a person brings home each year.

Technical Analysis – Analysis of securities based on the study of price movement using charts or graphs. This differs from fundamental analysis in that the intrinsic value of the security is not used.

Ticker Symbol – An arrangement of characters (or numbers) that represent a specific security listed on a stock exchange available for public trade.

Trading – Buying and selling financial securities such as stocks, bonds, mutual funds, and ETFs. Trading is different than investing in that the securities are usually held for a short period of time (seconds to several months). When investing, investors usually hold securities for many months to potentially decades.

Traditional IRA – A tax advantaged retirement investing account. A traditional IRA is tax-deferred (tax is paid when money is withdrawn at retirement age).

Trailing Stop Order – A stop order that can be set at a certain percentage away or a fixed amount from the security's current market price. These types of orders are meant to lock in gains if the security price suddenly shifts in an unprofitable direction. If the security continues to increase in value, then the trade remains open and the stop is adjusted automatically.

Treasury Bills (T-Bills) – Bonds issued by the US Government which have a duration of one year or less. These are sold in denominations of $1,000.

Value Stocks – A stock that trades at a lower price compared to what the fundamentals (dividends, earnings, value of assets, etc.) dictate for the fair market price. These are basically viewed as passed over "bargain stocks."

Yield – The annual dividend per share divided by the current stock price and expressed as a percentage. Yield is also known as the dividend return. For example, if a company pays $1 in dividends annually and the stock price is currently $50, then the yield is 2% ($1/$50).

www.ingramcontent.com/pod-product-compliance
Lightning Source LLC
Chambersburg PA
CBHW051214170526
45166CB00005B/1891